IMAGES OF ENGLAND

LEEDS
CINEMAS

OrangeMaid

The 'drink-on-a-stick'

Great Star of the cinema
and biggest sales-winner
for years

*

Get your share of
these big extra sales—
sell *OrangeMaid* now!

Double
the take

with

HOSTESS

THE ICE CREAM
WITH *added* CREAM
FOR *added* SALES

IMAGES OF ENGLAND

LEEDS CINEMAS

ROBERT E. PREEDY

TEMPUS

Frontispiece: *Two advertisements from 1957 encouraging cinema owners to boost their income through sales of ice cream and 'drink on a stick' ice lollies.*

First published 2005

Tempus Publishing Limited
The Mill, Brimscombe Port,
Stroud, Gloucestershire, GL5 2QG
www.tempus-publishing.com

British Library Cataloguing in Publication Data.
A catalogue record for this book is available from the British Library.

ISBN 0 7524 3583 3

Typesetting and origination by Tempus Publishing Limited.
Printed in Great Britain.

Contents

Acknowledgements

Tony Atkinson, Keith Briggs, Bob Hill, Brian Megson, Geoff J. Mellor, Steven Moore, Charles Morris, Tony Moss, Peter Osborn, Edgar Pickles, David Raby, Chris Ringwood, David M. Ryder, Jim Schultz, Leonard Segelman, Roger Spence, Geoff Thompson, Alan Thornton, Derrick Todd, Kevin Wheelan, Richard Whincup, David Williamson, Cinema Theatre Association, Garforth Local History Society, Yorkshire Post Newspapers and Leeds Central Library.

Chapter six is partly based on a magazine article, 'The Picture Palaces of Leeds – A Jewish Perspective', by Ronnie Miller.

Keith Briggs provided research material on the Cansfield circuit and would welcome extra information about the Clifton, Dominion and Savoy cinemas.

Introduction

Why do people go to the pictures? Sociologists offer us a number of reasons: to be transported into another life or time period; to escape from ordinary and mundane everyday life; to join a community of like-minded members; to enjoy some privacy away from the rest of the family.

Today we can add another reason: boredom with television. TV in the 1950s caused the demise of thousands of cinemas. Now after half a century of viewing we realise that a constant flow of the same ideas and themes has produced only an indifference to the small screen. We look now to the cinema for a special entertainment event. Yet the cinema business is in turmoil. Major chains have been sold – mostly to venture capital companies whose bottom line is profit, not artistic endeavour. As a consequence audiences are returning to small community-based independent screens where film choice is more in tune with local tastes.

And yet Headingley's flagship independent, the Lounge, closed in January 2005, followed seven months later by the Cottage Road cinema. Their surprising demise certainly raised questions about the viability of a single-screen operation. Even more alarming was the recent closure of multiplexes in Sheffield and Hull. As movies create greater publicity of a type not seen since the golden age of the 1930s, what is really happening behind the screens?

Oversupply is the simple answer. Too many multiplexes were built in the boom years. As a new one opened it halved the take at the nearest rival. Equally, as the first new multiplex arrived it spelled the death of the traditional city centre screens. The small independents clustered around the suburbs had long gone and the remaining solo operations tend now to be in small towns well away from the fierce heat of a multiplex.

As with many aspects of the movie industry, evolution is a recurring theme. Cinemas that didn't modernise during the coming of sound found that their film supply of silents rapidly dried up. Suburban cinemas were the first casualties of the TV age as city centre chains held on to prints by giving longer runs to popular films. And then, twenty years ago, after decades of underinvestment, the city centre sites were faced with competition from glitzy American multiplexes.

The power of publicity as film stars Norma and Constance Talmadge pose for cameras outside the Lounge cinema, Headingley, in November 1922. With them are Leonard Denham, owner of the cinema, and the newly appointed Lord Mayor of Leeds, Ald. Frank Fountain. The purpose of the sisters' visit was to judge a competition to find a British actress to play second lead to Norma in her forthcoming film Within the Law. *Preliminary heats were filmed in numerous cities including Leeds. 80,000 girls entered the competition and the winner was Margaret Leahy from London. During the visit, Norma's latest film,* Smilin' Through, *was conveniently showing in cinemas nationwide. (National Museum of Photography, Film and Television, Bradford.)*

It's sometimes difficult to understand the economics of a multiplex. For most of the day they play films to a handful of customers, but the philosophy is that you are open when the public wishes to come – rather than the old system of adhering to a traditional timetable. A multiplex also needs a constant flow of patrons to keep a steady turnover of popcorn. Sales from confectionary and drinks apparently provide 80 per cent of net profits. For an independent operator the reverse is the case, with perhaps only 20 per cent of profits coming from this ancillary source.

The cinema business survives by adapting to new challenges. It mirrors Hollywood which is constantly researching demographics and trying to predict the future tempo of the world in the two years it takes to produce a film. Multiplexes have to make the film experience pleasurable by offering comfort, ease of access and plentiful parking. At the same time it's essential to maximise spending opportunities by giving huge prominence to a refreshment counter.

So as we travel from the 1890s to the present day, we observe constant evolution in the business – one that has survived an onslaught from wireless, television, video, DVD and satellite. Who can predict the future of cinema? Only you – by your willingness to be enticed to the biggest, the best, the most intriguing, the most daring or the most romantic film ever screened.

So step right up folks – the show is about to begin.

one

A brief history

The early cinemas in Leeds, like elsewhere, tended to utilise existing large meeting rooms. In the 1890s film shows were an added attraction at the major theatres. Camera pioneers made short vignettes of life in the city which were shown in-between the normal artists on a variety show. From these early beginnings entrepreneurs developed a new medium.

Many people experienced their first cinema shows in a former shop in Briggate. The shop was about to be demolished but an enterprising businessman took a short lease on Stead's old Pork Shop. Admission was 2d for adults, 1d for children and two films were shown. One was *Street Scenes in Paris* and the other was a comedy about a demon that could wave his cloak and make people disappear in a puff of smoke. A carbon arc system of projection was used but the movement on the screen, although bright, was jerky.

In 1895 there was also another novelty show in Briggate. Here a mock-up of a railway carriage allowed patrons to see the line and countryside via a projector and screen. The effect was similar to the opening to the TV pop show, *6.5 Special*, sixty years later.

The first purpose-built cinema further down Briggate was on the site of the present day Marks & Spencer store. The magnificent Picture House was opened in April 1911 by Provincial

This gothic monument looks like a church but it opened as a concert hall and variety theatre in July 1885 and featured regular circus performances. Later Sydney Carter of New Century Pictures hired the hall for film shows from April 1905 and within a year this was so successful the shows transferred full time to the Assembly Rooms. North British Animated Films then took over at the Coliseum before being bought by Gaumont in the 1930s. The venue became the Gaumont-Coliseum in October 1938 and was particularly known for its popular Saturday matinees. Uncle Len Thompson recalls having 2,000 children there each week – until ITV started, when numbers plummeted by 90 per cent. Closure of the Gaumont came in December 1961 after which bingo was played here until 1969. The building has subsequently been used as a theatre, a film studio (Kenny Everett's Captain Kremmen sketches were filmed here) and latterly as a nightclub and music venue.

Cinematograph history bites the dust as the old Gainsborough, and former Electrocord film studio, is demolished.

Cinematograph Theatres. After a name change to the Rialto, this was the venue for the sound sensation of *The Singing Fool*. However, it was not the first to experiment with sound pictures. Both the Scala and the Theatre de Luxe screened locally-made talking pictures. Their efforts may seem crude now, but certainly set the scene for a cinema revolution in 1929.

These early films were made in Domestic Street in Tom Palmer's Electrocord studio behind the Gainsborough cinema. In the studio was a hand-cranked camera with a simple backcloth and basic lighting. Here the artist would stand and be filmed miming to a gramophone record. Each film lasted about three minutes and one included two singers miming to a Layton and Johnson disc. Once completed the film would be shown at Tom Palmer's Theatre de Luxe cinema, but synchronisation was always difficult as the film and sound disc had to be started at the same time. Palmer also manufactured Brunswick Panatropes – the forerunner of radiograms. His chief projectionist, G.J. Robinson, installed many of these, as well as the Electrocord cinema equipment, all over the country. He recalls seeing *The Singing Fool* about 600 times.

The Scala was the base for sound experiments by Dr de Forest but these were soon superseded once the Rialto premiered Al Jolson's film.

Installation of the Rialto's new equipment had taken six weeks and it was one of only six cinemas in the country licensed for the system. An embargo was placed on further installation for a full year. The next sound cinema in Leeds was surprisingly the Crown in Tong Road.

Closure is imminent for the Rialto. It's the last week of Oh Mr Porter, *with a billboard for the final week featuring George Raft in* Woman Teaser.

The Singing Fool ran for ten weeks at the Rialto and was shown six times a day to accommodate the crowds stretching up Boar Lane and Bond Street. The projection team of Jimmy Scott, Walter Greenwood and Eric Atkinson wore out three sets of discs during the run, and also needed two copies of the film in case of breakdown. In spite of this phenomenal success the Rialto survived for only another ten years. It was eclipsed by the new Paramount and Ritz and closed in 1939.

Earlier in the century rapid change in the industry had seen intermittent film shows in the Coliseum, Cookridge Street. These became more regular once cinema pioneer Sydney Carter took over the Assembly Rooms.

One of the city's great surviving suburban cinemas, the Cottage Road, opened a year after the Briggate Picture House as the flicks craze grew in residential parts of Leeds.

After the First World War the Majestic in City Square took the cinema experience to new heights of luxury. Within the building were a large ballroom and an elegant dining room. It was built to the designs of Pascal Steinlet, whose work had included four theatres and thirty cinemas, including the Abbeydale in Sheffield.

Occasional film shows were also popular at unexpected venues. Eric Rhodes, later to run the Classic chain, booked the Leeds Town Hall for a twelve-day run of the film *The King of Kings* in October 1927. In the 1930s the 1,500-seater Belgrave Central Hall held 'kinema shows', while at the same time the short-lived Monseigneur cinema was opened by the Davis Circuit of Wardour Street, London.

The coming of sound stimulated a new frenzy of interest for film fans. New cinemas built in the dark days of the thirties teased patrons with a glimpse of Hollywood's dream world.

The imposing Paramount, opened in 1932, sat perfectly in the sturdy architectural lines of the new Headrow. Inside this super-cinema patrons were offered the most sumptuous surroundings and comfort – the ladies' powder room is always recalled with great affection. The sight of usherettes wearing trousers caused a real stir as the decadent dangers of Americanisation became headline news.

Associated British Cinemas opened their new Ritz on Vicar Lane within two years and also offered the highest standard of courtesy and comfort. Male attendants wore dinner jackets and the chief of staff was resplendent in full tails.

During the war cinema attendances boomed and reached a peak of 1,450 million attendances in 1946 (compared with a low point of 54 million in 1984). BBC Television had screened its first feature film, *The Student of Prague*, in August 1938 and by 1949 was showing 173.

TV in the cinema was thought to be a solution and when the Telecinema opened for the 1951 Festival of Britain, it was a sensation. TV facilities were installed at the Leeds Odeon and the News Theatre but were little used after that.

Once ITV began in 1956 the cinema decline continued. When Granada scheduled *Wagon Train* on a Monday evening, cinema audiences plummeted and the rest of the week suffered from lack of word of mouth advertising.

However, optimism remained within the industry and both ABC and Rank built a number of new cinemas in the late 1950s and early '60s. In Leeds the Odeon Merrion Centre opened as a 'Roadshow' house screening extended runs of broad appeal films. Cinerama shows came here within a few years, but by then the golden age of cinema-going had come to an end. Increasing affluence, universal TV ownership and a fragmented market meant that the weekly habit of enjoying a picture was lost to millions.

The Merrion Centre Odeon ran from 1964 for just thirteen years. With hindsight it opened at the wrong time in the wrong place – although the film experience for customers was second to none.

An advertising feature from the Yorkshire Evening Post *publicises the opening of the Odeon Merrion cinema in August 1964.*

The final week of the Odeon as it screened the unforgettable Vivien Leigh classic, Gone With the Wind.

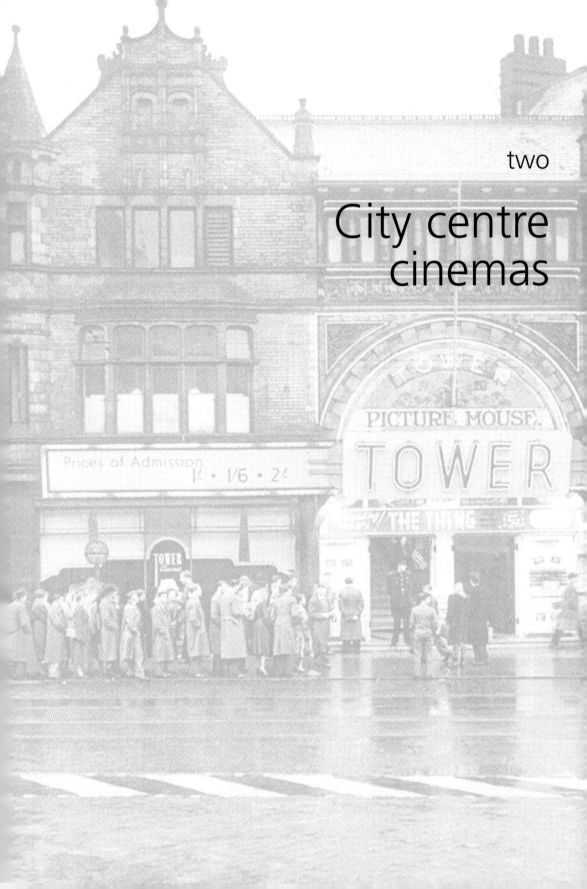

two

City centre cinemas

ASSEMBLY ROOMS (1907-1985)

Built in the vast complex consisting of the Grand Theatre and a parade of shops, the Assembly Rooms were first used for film shows in 1907 by Sydney Carter when he transferred his New Century films from the Coliseum.

The name was changed to the Plaza when Star Cinemas took over and they continued with an increasingly saucy line-up until closure in 1985. Since then the auditorium has become a rehearsal room for the Grand Theatre, although the projectors are still up in the box.

Opposite: *Part of the Grand Theatre building, the Assembly Rooms/Plaza survived on X-rated fare for many years. The memoirs of a Plaza manager or projectionist are long overdue.*

Right and below: *The ornate interior of the Assembly Rooms/Plaza perhaps gave cinema enthusiasts an excuse to buy a ticket and study the architecture. But would the wife believe it?*

Above: *The attractive frontage leading up to the Tatler – a cinema that in its time provided entertainment and stimulation for the discerning cinemagoer.*

Left: *The final advert for the much missed Tatler.*

THEATRE DE LUXE (1910-1934)

Tom Palmer's Theatre de Luxe in Kirkgate was a remodelled confectioner's shop. Although much has changed since closure in 1934, it is still possible to make out the frontage. The cinema owner was keen on innovation and started producing pioneering short sound films at the Electrocord studios in Holbeck from 1927.

PICTURE HOUSE, BRIGGATE (1911-1939)

This central cinema was the first major development in the city by a national chain. Provincial Cinematograph Theatres leased the building for their stylish Picture House which opened in 1911. Inside were Wedgwood and Jacobean tea lounges and a smoking room for gentlemen. Magazines and newspapers were provided for patrons and membership of an exclusive cinema club was also offered.

The coming of sound created a sensation when the Rialto (as the Picture House was known from February 1927) screened *The Singing Fool* for an unprecedented ten weeks from 11 March to 11 May 1927. But even with this momentum the cinema was soon to be overshadowed by the Paramount and the Ritz. The Picture House was sold for redevelopment in 1939 and after the Second World War a new Marks & Spencer store was built on the site.

CITY (1915-1964)

Inside the Royal Exchange Chambers on Boar Lane from 1915 was the City cinema. It tended to offer a specialised programme, especially in the 1920s and '30s when it was home to foreign films. While mainstream audiences could easily find the blockbusters, the Tatler screened handpicked classics and works of art – films like *La Ronde*, *Infidelity* and *The Seven Deadly Sins*.

The cinema had various names – the Savoy, the Academy and, from 1936, the Tatler News Theatre. It shortened its name to just Tatler once the News Theatre opened in City Square two years later. Although many patrons thought the sight lines were appalling the cinema survived for fifty years, not closing until 1964 when the entire building was redeveloped into the present day Royal Exchange House.

TOWER (1920-1985)

A growing chain of Yorkshire cinemas was increased when they bought the lease of part of the Grand Arcade and turned it into their latest picture house, the Tower, opening in 1920. As the decade came to an end the Tower defiantly declared itself the stronghold of silents; 'Talkies are not screened here, only the best silent pictures accompanied by a human orchestra under the direction of Bensley Ghent'. However, within a few months the supply of silents dried up and the Tower was converted to sound in March 1930.

After the opening of the super cinemas, the Paramount and Ritz, the Tower became a second-run hall, but when the picture was right it could outperform the majors. After the Second World War, when a flood of American pictures returned after the embargo, the Tower was able to pick up new films. The 1950 MGM film *Command Decision* became a huge hit here. On its first Sunday both houses were completely sold out.

The Tower was part of Associated Tower Cinemas Ltd who also had the Carlton, Cottage Road, Crescent, Pavilion in Stanningley and from 1970 the Lounge. After closure in 1985 the Tower's long-serving Victoria 4 projectors were sent to Guyana, while the seats were reused at Malton's cinema, reopened by Tony Atkinson, the final manager of Beeston's Malvern cinema.

Built in the Grand Arcade in 1920, the Tower could still attract crowds throughout its life. Here orderly queues of neatly dressed patrons await entry to The Thing *in October 1952.*

A new read-o-graph and sign greet a diminishing number of patrons at the Tower in 1970.

MAJESTIC (1922-1969)

Land for a new picture house was bought from the council for £80,000. A recruiting office had occupied the site during the war, but now entrepreneurs spotted the potential of a prominent cinema opposite the railway station. Once built the cinema seated 3,600 and the restaurant 300.

Leonard Denham was appointed General Manager of the Majestic Picture House and Restaurant. Denham was a busy gentleman – suburban audiences also knew him as the proprietor of the Lounge in Headingley, as well as other cinemas in Leeds and across Yorkshire.

The opening film came from the Empire in London where it had achieved a record run of 271 performances. D.W. Griffith's *Way Down East* was seen by 50,000 people in its first week at the Majestic and was naturally retained for a second week. For its third week patrons enjoyed the Norma Talmadge film *The Sign on the Door*, with the next film being Stewart Rome's *Penniless Millionaire*.

Notable events at the Majestic include a political rally addressed by David Lloyd George in October 1922. In 1932 the cinema became the first provincial hall to install deaf aids. *South Pacific* opened here in September 1958 and ran for thirty-eight weeks, being seen by half a million people. But even this record was broken by *The Sound of Music* which was screened for two and a half years from 1967 to 1969.

Under construction – the palatial Majestic in 1921.

The completed Majestic super cinema just after opening in 1922.

Centre and left: *Two interior pictures of the Majestic. What an atmosphere must have been created during a full house. Just in front of the stage, the orchestra pit and the organ.*

Waiting areas at the Majestic were also of a very high standard, creating a dreamlike vista for patrons.

Before or after the show, a visit to the Majestic restaurant was a must.

The Gaming Act, law from 30 September 1960, changed the economics of cinemas. The downturn in audiences made it an easy decision for owners to convert to bingo. In 1961 afternoon bingo started in the Majestic ballroom. For accuracy we record the first number called was 33 and the first prize £20!

By 1967 the game had become so popular that full-time bingo took over the ballroom. Within two years bingo also meant the end of film. The eight-year-old Gaumont club closed and bingo sessions transferred to the Majestic. The final film on 10 July 1969 was Clint Eastwood's *The Good, the Bad and the Ugly*. Later the building became the Majestyk nightclub, but it is shortly to house a giant casino.

SCALA THEATRE (1922-1957)

The Scala opened just three weeks after the Majestic and was built in the heart of Leeds' theatre land. Together with its ballroom, the Scala was a favourite with audiences for all its thirty-five years.

Staff at its opening in 1922 included manager William Greenfield and chief engineer George Lodge. Lodge had previously been a film producer and became well-known in Leeds for his newsreels of local events. Anton Tschaikov led the Scala orchestra.

Disney's *Snow White* had its Leeds premiere here and patrons heard Charlie Chaplin's first spoken words in the film *Monsieur Verdoux*.

The cinema was taken over by the Rank Organisation in the late 1940s and one of their first big shows was *Hamlet*, which played to capacity houses for nine weeks in 1948. In the mid-1950s *Rock Around the Clock* made its debut here, but luckily before the film gained notoriety among teenage vandals. The Scala was also used as the first Yorkshire venue for the BBC series, *A Seat in the Circle*.

Many of the staff at the Scala enjoyed long service. Some of the forty-five cinema staff had spent twenty-five years each with the company and were very sorry to leave the family atmosphere when the Scala closed in 1957. The building became a furniture showroom and is still used for retail today.

Top: *A new canopy giving a fresh look to the Scala cinema in the 1950s.*

Above: *The fabulous interior of Yorkshire's wonder cinema – the Scala, 1922-1957.*

Right: *Doorman Vincent Johnson signs off at the final show at the Scala.*

Opposite: *The Scala pictured in September 1949.*

Mr. Vincent Johnson
—today's Y.E. News picture.

PARAMOUNT (1932-1998)

Eager crowds streamed along the Headrow on the Gala opening night of the American-backed Paramount Theatre – the epitome of Hollywood here in Leeds. Luxury was the byword with the most comfortable seats and contemporary design. The Paramount seated over 2,500 and must have affected business at existing cinemas but such was the demand for cinema that no major ones closed during the decade.

In 1940 the Paramount chain was sold to the Odeon group and one of the conditions of the sale was that original American equipment must always be used. The projectors thus gave sterling service from 1932 until 1963 when the lack of spare parts forced a change to Kalee.

In 1952 the Odeon played host to a replica Royal Film Performance of Mario Lanza's *Because You're Mine*. A special train brought a host of stars to Leeds including Jack Hawkins, Maurice Denham, Guy Middleton, Petula Clark and James Hayter. A crowd of 6,000 greeted them as they entered the Odeon for this special night.

As audiences declined through the 1960s, the cinema was twinned to offer greater film choice. From reopening in 1969 both Odeon 1 (the circle) and 2 (the old stalls) were equipped for 70mm projection, but only one such film was ever shown in Odeon 2 – *Close Encounters of the Third Kind*. The projectionists remember with gloom their three shows a day of this lengthy movie.

After twinning the old café and restaurant became a bar before conversion to Odeon 3, opening in July 1978 and also showing *Close Encounters*!

Odeon 3 was later renamed 5, after the rear stalls of 2 were twinned into 3 and 4. Once plans were announced to build the 'Light' multiplex on the Headrow, the Odeon was under threat and closed seven months before competition arrived. The Odeon's business had already been hit by the opening of the Warner multiplex in 1998 – so rather than wait for another fight, the building was put up for sale – just two years after the nearby ABC had closed.

The Headrow was redeveloped along these clean lines and the Paramount was the star at the centre. Here it is in its first week.

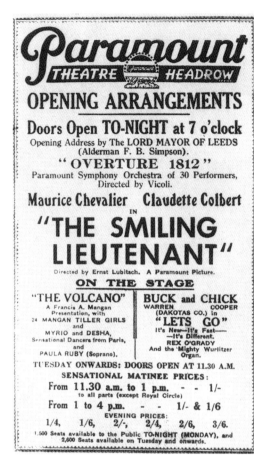

• • • *The 1952 Replica Royal Film Performance* • • •

THE ODEON - LEEDS

Programme

★ **STANLEY TUDOR**

The popular Broadcasting Organist at the ODEON Wurlitzer

★ **"BECAUSE YOU'RE MINE"**

THE CAST

Renaldo Rossano	Mario Lanza
Bridget Batterson	Dorretta Morrow
Sgt. Batterson	James Whitmore
Ben Jones	Dean Miller
Francesca Landers	Paula Corday
Patty Ware	Jeff Donnell
Mrs. Motville	Spring Byington
Gen. Montville	Curtis Cooksey
Capt. Burton Nordell Loring	Don Porter
Albert Parkson Foster	Eduard Franz
Artie Pilcer	Bobby Van
Horsey	Ralph Reed
Mrs. Rossano	Celia Lovsky
Maestro Paradori	Alexander Steinert

★ **MEET THE STARS**

Great Stage Presentation — Produced by JOHN VARLEY

★ **GERALDO AND HIS CONCERT ORCHESTRA**

The Famous Broadcaster and his Orchestra

★ **THE YORKSHIRE SINGERS**

Presented by and under the direction of H.BARDGETT, Esq., O.B.E., Mus. Bac., F.R.C.O.

★ **NANCY EVANS**

The Famous Mezzo-Soprano Concert Artist

God Save The Queen

STAGE DIRECTION by JACK PRENDERGAST, M.B.E.

Above: *Programme for the 1952 Royal Film permormance at the Odeon, Leeds.*

Right: *Details of the attractions on opening day at the Paramount, Monday 22 February 1932.*

Below: *The splendid staircase up to the balcony of the Paramount.*

Paramount
THEATRE HEADROW

OPENING ARRANGEMENTS

Doors Open TO-NIGHT at 7 o'clock

Opening Address by The LORD MAYOR OF LEEDS
(Alderman F. B. Simpson).

"OVERTURE 1812"

Paramount Symphony Orchestra of 30 Performers,
Directed by Vicoli.

Maurice Chevalier   Claudette Colbert
IN

"THE SMILING LIEUTENANT"

Directed by Ernst Lubitsch. A Paramount Picture.

ON THE STAGE

"THE VOLCANO"	BUCK and CHICK
A Francis A. Mangan Presentation, with 24 MANGAN TILLER GIRLS and MYRIO and DESHA, Sensational Dancers from Paris, and PAULA RUBY (Soprano).	WARREN COOPER (DAKOTAS CO.) in "LETS GO" It's New—It's Fast— —It's Different. REX O'GRADY And the Mighty Wurlitzer Organ.

TUESDAY ONWARDS: DOORS OPEN AT 11.30 A.M.

SENSATIONAL MATINEE PRICES:

From 11.30 a.m. to 1 p.m. - - 1/-
to all parts (except Royal Circle)

From 1 to 4 p.m. - - 1/- & 1/6

EVENING PRICES:

1/4,   1/6,   2/-,   2/4,   2/6,   3/6.

1,500 Seats available to the Public TO-NIGHT (MONDAY), and
2,600 Seats available on Tuesday and onwards.

Inside the projection box at the Odeon – the light source for our cinema dreams.

Opposite above, left and right: *Greeting the crowds at the Paramount in 1932 were ushers Phyllis Holmes and Frank Cooper. The usherettes' brown trouser suits caused much comment.*

Opposite below left: *Projectionist Roger Spence carefully threads the film. Roger was at the Odeon from 1954 to 1963. These days his training and skills are put to good use at the Wetherby Film Theatre.*

Opposite below right: *A TV system was installed for the Coronation and later used to screen live coverage of this 1954 football match.*

The interior of the Odeon just prior to twinning in 1969. This was the balcony view enjoyed by millions since the Paramount opened thirty-seven years earlier.

Reconstruction during twinning shows the top part of the original proscenium. The former balcony was extended forward to form Odeon 1.

Above and left: *The completed project showing the care and attention that retained a traditional feel to Odeon 1.*

Above and left: *In the former stalls, Odeon 2 also looks extremely attractive.*

The Odeon exterior just a few months after the internal twinning.

Odeon 3, a 126-seat mini cinema, was created in the former café/restaurant/bar area.

RITZ (1934-2000)

The Ritz opened to great acclaim in 1934 and became the sixty-sixth cinema then in Leeds. It consisted of one million bricks and took ten months to construct. Once opened the Ritz employed forty-five staff – the front of house staff all wearing very smart dark green whipcord. The male ushers wore dinner jackets, and the ladies had matching shade frocks. The chief of staff impressed in full dress tails.

Lewis Gerard was the cinema's first player on the Compton organ, impressively illuminated in a rainbow of colours. The wizard of the keys had come from the Empire in Coventry and made his first BBC broadcast from here at the Ritz in January 1935.

Two months later organist Nelson Elms took over, later followed by Clifford Birchall. The Compton was removed from the Ritz in 1968 and is fully restored in a private house in Markfield, Leicestershire.

Fifteen-year-old Joan Lodge was one of the first usherettes and remembers joining the massive queue for jobs. 'Mr Butler, the chief of staff, was very strict. Each morning there was an inspection of our hands, nails, uniforms and shoes. We all had to be immaculate – even though our pay was just thirty shillings for a very long week. We also had to wear large exotic hats. Later they decided that all the usherettes should be blondes. That cost me 1s 6d at the hairdressers!'

Gone with the Wind began a record six-week run at the Ritz from 16 November 1942 and the same film closed the Odeon, Merrion Centre in October 1977. The ABC was twinned in 1970 and became a triple cinema from March 1974.

When the Warners multiplex opened in 1998 the ABC cut admission prices, but with little effect. This traditional city centre cinema closed two years later.

The Ritz cinema on Vicar Lane.

Prior to the underpass being built, the ABC was next to this ornate building.

The new look Cannon, covering up the original facings, but presenting a contemporary view to Vicar Lane.

Inside the new ABC 1, built in the former circle.

This lower projection box covered both the smaller ABC screens, 2 and 3.

NEWS THEATRE (1938-1981)

To entertain passengers waiting at the station, the News Theatre was incorporated into the Queen's Hotel. It offered a continuous performance of shorts, cartoons and newsreels so customers could dip in and out of the programme.

In the early 1950s the News Theatre, like the Odeon, installed a TV screen to show live pictures of the Coronation.

The News Theatre had many name changes in its life. It became the Classic in 1966 and the Tatler Classic Club in 1969, reverting to the Classic again ten years later. Sex films predominated for its latter two decades as the cinema struggled to find a regular audience.

The Classic closed in 1981 after screening its final film, *Sex Life in a Convent*, but reopened three months later for a two-week festival of art films. The 'Screen in the Square' was operated by Ambassador Cinemas of Oulton. The previous year they had tried to reopen the Merrion Centre Odeon and later controlled cinemas in Huddersfield and Malton until they were forced into bankruptcy. The City Square venture was also less successful than expected and the old News Theatre eventually became a nightclub. One of the projectors was positioned over the bar as a reminder of earlier times.

Left and opposite: *Interior shots of the News Theatre prior to opening in 1938.*

Above: *The last reel of the final film at the Classic, January 1981.*

Left: *The programme from the 'Screen in the Square' film festival.*

Festival of Film 1987

formerly Classic Cinema
City Square, Leeds 1

May 16th — GALA NIGHT   ANIMAL FARM/RUDDIGORE
Two Halas & Batchelor animated cartoons, both excellent examples of British cinema.
Animal Farm, the first operetta to be treated in animation.
Tickets for this performance cost £4.00 and are excluded from the Festival Ticket. We
will have a full display of production material for Animal Farm, and it is hoped that both
John Halas and Joy Batchelor will both be present for this Gala opening. The Gala Night
is in aid of the Festival Chorus.

May 17th — Sunday **DIE NIEBELUNGEN**
Fritz Lang's silent epic based on the Nordic legends. There will
be piano accompaniment for this performance.

May 18th — Monday **THE LIFE OF ANTON BRUCKNER**
A compelling and dramatic film about the life and music of
Bruckner.

May 19th — Tuesday **THE RED SHOES**
A rare chance to see the famous British production, with a
superlative cast.

May 20th — Wednesday **A MAN FOR ALL SEASONS**
Robert Bolt's production of the life of Sir Thomas More, with
Paul Scofield in the title role.

May 21st — Thursday **BEGGARS OPERA/BLITHE SPIRIT**
Screened at 2.00pm & 6.30pm
Beggar's Opera, a classic film of the fifties, starring Laurence
Olivier and Dorothy Tutin. Blithe Spirit, starring Noël Coward
and Margaret Rutherford.

May 22nd — Friday **THE GREAT MR. HANDEL**
A moving and inspirational account of Handel's life and
writing of The Messiah.

Friday — Late Night **A KING'S STORY**
10.30pm
The dramatic and moving account of Edward VIII's marriage to
Mrs. Simpson and the Abdication. Made in the sixties, with
comments and reflections by the Duke and Duchess of Windsor.

May 23rd — Saturday **MY FAIR LADY**
Another chance to enjoy this all time favourite on the big screen.

May 24th — Sunday **HENRY V**
Laurence Olivier's memorable film with music by William Walton.

May 25th — Monday **THE MAGIC FLUTE**
Ingmar Bergman's magical production of this Mozart opera.

May 26th — Tuesday **THINGS TO COME**
Alexander Korda's remarkable film of Britain in the near future,
again with a classic film score by William Walton.

May 27th — Wednesday **FIDELIO/ANIMAL FARM**
Presented here are two films showing the different sides of
oppression. Walter Felsenstein's unique film of the Beethoven
opera, with Magda Laszlo; and another chance to see the Halas
and Batchelor production of George Orwell's Animal Farm.

May 28th — Thursday **THE FINEST HOURS**
Jack Le Vien's stunning and moving film about the life of
Winston Churchill, culminating with the end of the second
World War.

May 29th — Friday **SCOTT OF THE ANTARCTIC**
This, film starring John Mills in one of his most famous roles, is
also one of the all time favourites of British cinema. The score is
by Vaughan Williams.

May 30th — Saturday **ROMEO AND JULIET**
Paul Conner's beautiful production of Prokofieff's ballet, starring
Rudolph Nureyev and Margot Fonteyn.

BOOKING INFORMATION

SEAT PRICES:		Special Reductions for School
ADULTS	£1.40p	Parties during matinee
CHILDREN	60p	performances.
O.A.P.'s (matinees only)	50p	Film Festival Ticket (for all
STUDENTS (with S.U. Card)	£1.00p	14 performances) only £10.

All seats bookable in advance

All screenings begin at 2.00pm and 7.00pm, unless otherwise stated.

For further information telephone Leeds 823896/456133/457284 or write to Ambassador Cinema
Company, 25 Parkways Avenue, Oulton.

We regret that due to circumstances totally beyond our control, we have had to cancel our
screening of Joseph Losey's film "DON GIOVANNI".

ODEON MERRION (1964-1977)

Described in 1964 as the 'Super cinema of the Seventies', the Merrion Centre Odeon was the first new cinema to open in Leeds since the Rex in 1939. It was built within the city's first giant shopping complex, the Merrion Centre and for its first eight years the cinema was on the roadside, with a regular bus service passing its doors.

Seating 900, this was Rank's answer to falling attendances. It was planned to eventually replace the ageing Majestic but Fox Pictures insisted that *South Pacific* play at the Majestic – a two and half year run that would certainly have secured the future of the Merrion Centre.

The new Odeon was the height of luxury and comfort with a special heating system that gently circulated warm air from below the screen to an extractor above the projection box. Narrow heating pipes also ran under all the seats to give extra warmth during the winter.

A sound system covered the auditorium with a dozen speakers positioned through the length of the ceiling. The foyer had luxury leather seats set below a giant chandelier. Patrons entered the auditorium up central stairs and could sit either in the upper balcony section or the lower stalls. The giant 50ft curved screen was positioned within a 62ft screen frame and the view from the stalls was an IMAX-type experience.

The Odeon in the Merrion Centre was built for the heyday of 'roadshow presentations' – huge spectacular epics that could run for months in one cinema. The opening film here was *The Fall of the Roman Empire* and the cinema drew capacity crowds for many years with this type of film. The closure for twinning of the Headrow Odeon gave the Merrion Centre a business boost for nine months.

Also in 1969 a new Cinerama system was installed in Rank cinemas across the country. This was a three-projector invention that gave immaculate definition on the giant screen. However, the join between the three images often distracted from the presentation.

By the time the Merrion Centre Odeon was fitted with the system, it had been modified to a solo 70mm projector under the name of Ultra-Panavision. Although not strictly Cinerama, it was advertised as such and did give a spectacular screen image. The first such film, *Ice Station Zebra*, was screened here from 10 July 1969 but a shortage of films meant that only two more were shown in this format; *Grand Prix* and the final Cinerama film, *2001: A Space Odyssey*. Incidentally also on the 10 July, bingo at the Gaumont ended and the Majestic cinema closed to become a bingo hall – a busy day in the Rank calendar.

The seventies saw more contraction of cinema audiences and the Merrion Centre found itself competing for films with the Headrow Odeon. Also, from 1972, expansion of the shopping complex meant the Odeon was now inside the centre rather than on the exterior, as a new roof was added and the public highway became a pedestrian link through the shops. Rank tried to have a new sign positioned on the outside of the centre but planners turned down the request.

For its final five years the cinema survived on offbeat and specialised films that drew a small, but very appreciative, audience. Sadly appreciation doesn't pay the bills and the Odeon was forced to close in October 1977 with an appropriate film, *Gone with the Wind*. This single screen city centre cinema had become outdated history by 1969 when the modernised twin Odeon, Headrow, reopened.

There have been many plans to reopen the cinema and the Rank Organisation was more than willing to offload the remains of their twenty-one-year lease. Although the projection equipment was soon removed (to the Odeon in Coventry), the seats and screen remained until November 1984.

The last attempt to resurrect the cinema was in 2004 when a consortium almost reached a deal, but pulled out when a survey showed that compliance with current building regulations would cost £1 million.

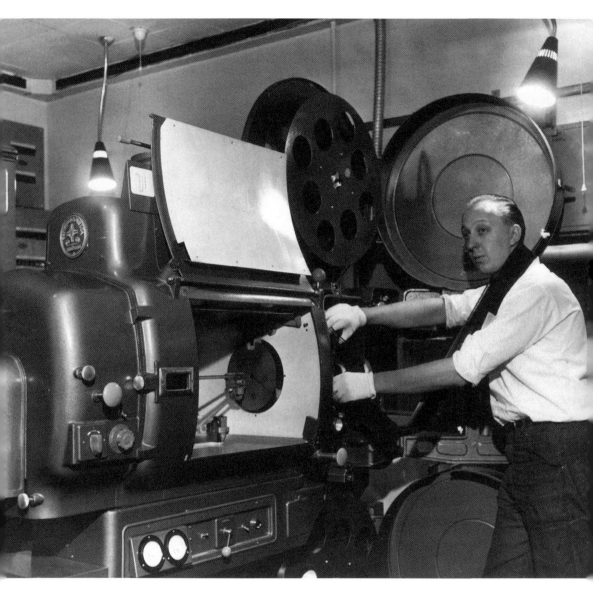

Chief Projectionist Jack Lambert checks the print at the Merrion prior to opening. At this stage there was no water supply, so with dirty hands Jack protects the film with white gloves.

Left: *Adding the Odeon lettering just prior to opening of the Merrion Centre Cinema.*

Left and below: *The simple but clean lines of the Merrion Centre auditorium – a first class viewing experience.*

It's not mad to shop at Tesco, enjoy a movie and then catch a bus home.

Song of Norway – one of the long running films that should have secured a bright future for the new Odeon.

The attractive foyer showing the ticket kiosk, the candy bar and the auditorium entrance at the Odeon.

Thirteen years for the newest cinema in town — then gone with the wind.

THE ODEON
MERRION CENTRE
IS NOW CLOSED

ALL ENQUIRIES PLEASE TO
THE ODEON · HEADROW
Tel: 30031

The last picture show has ended.

PLAYHOUSE FILM THEATRE (1970-1990)

The Playhouse Theatre was always closed on a Sunday until a film society was formed to show foreign and art movies. Being close to the university, it quickly found a regular audience and a full house was the norm for most of its life. When the new West Yorkshire Playhouse was built on the former Quarry Hill flats site, films ceased and the original theatre became a conference centre. All the cinema equipment remains and is occasionally used for corporate and advertising presentations.

Left and below: *The Playhouse Theatre, exterior and interior.*

three

Suburban cinemas

Headingley

COTTAGE ROAD (1912-PRESENT)

At the cinema's seventieth birthday celebrations in 1982, many former members of staff were invited to a special showing of *Chariots of Fire*. Among the guests was Gertrude Lyons, who played the piano for the children's matinees here from 1923. She confessed to have little musical training but could play by ear. She recalled with great affection the boisterous youngsters and their excitement for the cowboy films. Sixty years on she could also recall the smell of orange peel. Throughout the week Gertrude was the cashier and for all those hours she received a weekly pay of £1. Other regulars remembered serials like *The Perils of Pauline* and the agonising wait until next Saturday to see the outcome of the cliff-hanger.

The doorkeeper was keen on cleanliness and particularly proud of the new carpets and told patrons to clean their boots before entering the premises.

The cinema started life as a garage, built on the site of old stables. The garage was quickly converted to a cinema in 1912 but many residents expressed concern about the queues and nightly noise. However, once open the cinema proved popular and during the First World War news flashes were shown on the screen.

In 1972 major renovations took place bringing the seating capacity down to 468. Newer Victoria 9 projectors came in 1981 from the Grove, Smethwick.

The Cottage Road cinema is part of the Associated Tower Cinema group, who previously had two cinemas in Ripon, together with a number in Leeds. Their decision to close the Lounge in 2005 put a question mark over the long-term viability of the Cottage Road cinema. The number of customers who support the cinema will, as always, have the final say, and this, the oldest cinema in Leeds, was sadly closed by the company in July 2005.

Opposite, above and below: *The exterior, kiosk and interior of the Cottage Road cinema. Note the former Lounge seats.*

HYDE PARK (1913-PRESENT)

Henry Child, owner of the Mitre Hotel in Commercial Street, originally built the Hyde Park in 1906. However a licence was refused by the council and after alterations it opened as the Brudenell Road Social and Recreation Club. Eventually in 1913 the premises were converted into the Hyde Park Picture House. Business was so successful that two Saturday performances were always fully booked up.

By the 1950s the cinema business was in rapid decline and the Hyde Park, like many others was forced to close. However, as in the Saturday serials, a disaster is always averted. Leslie Shann took over within a few months and ran it until 1957, when even his fresh enthusiasm was not enough.

Within five years another saviour rode into view. This was a familiar face to thousands of matinee-goers at the Gaumont – Len Thompson. He took over in 1962 and quickly refurbished the place, installing BTH projectors from the recently closed Savoy, Lupset. The cinema ran successfully by placing special emphasis on the growing student audiences in the area. After Len's death in August 1977, his nephew Geoff took over and was here until 1993. Geoff was no newcomer to the business – at age nine he was an attendant at the Gaumont and by sixteen was projectionist at his uncle's cinema, the Crown in Tong Road.

The exterior of the Hyde Park cinema.

*Geoff Thompson, Hyde Park's
dedicated manager for sixteen years.*

*The Edwardian foyer of the Hyde
Park Picture House showing the
stairs to the balcony.*

*Inside the Hyde Park Picture
House, still partly lit by gas.*

LOUNGE (1916-2005)

The Lounge Kinema was opened in the middle of the First World War by Middlesbrough entrepreneur Charles Metcalfe. However, shortly afterwards he concluded that the war would drag on and he signed sale papers in the trenches. It was taken over by Leeds and District Picture Houses, owned by Harry Hylton, Leonard Denham and brothers Miles and William Read.

The Lounge organ was installed in 1919 and ran with an orchestra for many years. Ross projectors ran smoothly from 1947 to 1982 when newer Victoria 8s were bought from the Odeon Grimsby. These have recently been transferred to the Hyde Park cinema.

Once the Warner multiplex opened in the summer of 1998, the future of the Lounge was cast into doubt. In virtually every other case like this, the independent has cut and run to avoid a slow and painful demise.

However, the Lounge was defiant. 'We are different from the Warners and Showcase. There is a theatrical, almost showbiz ambience at the Lounge. That is something our patrons enjoy and keep coming back for.' These words echoed those from manager David Williamson over thirty years earlier; 'If you can combine a friendly atmosphere and give patrons what they want then the suburban cinema will survive and flourish.'

The local newspaper carried out a comparison between the Lounge and Warners with the worrying conclusion, 'the brash new kid beats old world charmer on sound, comfort and leg room.'

Within months it was reported the Lounge was losing up to 65 per cent of its weekend business but surprisingly two years later £700,000 was spent on renovations and upgrading. A further £20,000 went on sound and subtitling equipment. Sadly all this was to no avail. Audiences continued to slide. Once the Warners was rebranded as Vue with a more mature image, the final battle scene began.

The Lounge's traditional older audience was now offered a similar experience just a mile away in Kirkstall. Losses at the Lounge mounted for five years and decisive action had to be taken.

On Friday 7 January 2005 the week's new film, *Alexander*, was spooled up and ready to run but none of the staff had any inkling that their final Thursday night had gone by without ceremony.

Petitions and letters of protest were sent to the local newspaper, but within days equipment, seating and carpeting had been sold – much of it to the council-owned Hyde Park cinema half a mile away. Advertising for the Lounge continued until Monday 10 January, even mentioning the film *Closer* to preview Thursday at 5.40 p.m. with a full run from Friday 14 January.

The now closed Lounge – once known as the North Lane Picture Lounge – with the listings for the final shows on Thursday 6 January 2005.

Above: *Leonard Denham – Managing Director of the Lounge and many other cinemas.*

Right: *James Parker, the efficient manager of the Lounge through the 1920s*

Below: *The traditional but contemporary interior of the Lounge – now sadly lost to cinemagoers.*

The Electra Picture Lounge.

Manager V.L. Winterburn with the staff of the Carlton Cinema in 1951.

Woodhouse

ELECTRA (1916-1957)

This was built in a former church and opened in 1916. Before its demolition a decade ago, a number of posters could still be seen on the walls. The Electra Lounge closed in 1957 and became a clothing factory.

Little London

CARLTON (1920-1965)

The Carlton later became part of the Associated Tower group, but was opened in 1920 by London and General Theatres Ltd – rather a small enterprise for such a grandly named company. By the mid-1960s housing changes in the area diminished its audience and the Carlton closed in 1965.

V.L. Winterburn.

The interior of the Carlton.

CAPITOL (1922-1968)

The Capitol was ahead of its time, being a multi-purpose entertainment complex. It housed a 1,300-seat cinema, a huge ballroom, a billiard hall and a number of shops. It proved a huge success from opening in 1922 and became an Associated Tower cinema in 1934. During the war the ballroom was always packed for its weekend shows and private bookings during the week made it a very busy venue. Sadly though, the familiar call of bingo took over in 1968 and the premises were finally demolished in 1980.

Left: *The prosperous Capitol in 1956.*

Opposite, above, left: *A 1964 advert for the Capitol cinema.*

Opposite, above, right: *Manager Douglas Thackrah in front of the screen before the final show on Saturday 27 January 1968. During the day 200 children had queued for the last matinee performance.*

Opposite below: *The demolition of the Capitol in 1980.*

THE
CAPITOL
CINEMA

MEANWOOD — **LEEDS 6**

Telephone **5 4 4 4 0**

Manager : S. JACKSON

ADMISSION PRICES :
CIRCLE - **2/6**
STALLS - **2/0**

Children under 14 years
(except Sats., Suns. and Holidays)
CIRCLE 2/0   STALLS 1/3

CONTINUOUS
Mon. to Sat. from 5.45 p.m. approx.
Sundays from 5.0 p.m. approx.

CAR PARK FOR PATRONS

The Management reserve the right to
alter the advertised programme

NOVEMBER 1964

The stone exterior of the Dominion in its bingo days.

The renovated interior of the Dominion in 1953.

Chapel Allerton

DOMINION (1934-1967)

This was the first of three suburban cinemas built in Leeds by the Bradford building company Cansfield's. The interest had started for quarry owner Albert Cansfield and his younger brother Lambert when they slowly became part owners of some Bradford cinemas, the Birch Lane (from 1914), Lyceum (1919), Carlton (1922), and the Cosy (1930). During this austere decade they branched out into Leeds where their stylish trio of cinemas was designed by Bradford architect William Illingworth. His pedigree was impeccable, having drawn plans for the Prince's Hall, Shipley (1911), Saltaire Picture House (1922) and the magnificent New Victoria (later the Gaumont/Odeon) in 1930.

Cansfield's first Leeds project was on a new housing estate at Chapel Allerton. Many of the street names had Canadian origins and on Montreal Avenue they erected the Dominion Super Cinema. After its opening on Thursday 4 January 1934, the local newspaper described it as 'spacious, lofty and well contrived – in fact one of the best cinemas in Leeds'. The cinema seated nearly 1600 and was equipped with a full stage and dressing rooms.

During the war a fire broke out one evening in June 1941. Within hours the roof collapsed, destroying the auditorium, but because of building restrictions renovation wasn't attempted until twelve years later, by which time West Leeds Amusements had bought the site. A grand reopening took place on Monday 21 December 1953 with the film *By the Light of the Silvery Moon* starring Doris Day and Gordon Macramé.

Within a year the Dominion became the first Leeds suburban cinema to install Cinemascope equipment and opened with *Flight of the White Heron* from 14 June 1954. Due to a dispute between Rank and Fox films, the Dominion became the Leeds outlet for subsequent scope pictures, until the central Tower cinema shared this honour from September.

Cansfield's other two cinemas in Leeds were the Savoy, Stanningley and Bramley's Clifton.

Chapeltown

FORUM (1936-1959)

The Forum opened in 1936 and specialised in Yiddish films for the large Jewish population in the suburb of Chapeltown. MP Gerald Kaufman recalls such delights as *Yiddel with a Fiddle* and *French Lesson*, about a teacher who knew no French but instead taught Yiddish to unsuspecting pupils. An organ was a feature of the cinema and the BBC player Len Bermon was the first musician.

By 1950 lessee Gerald Segelman tired of the cinema and handed it over to his brothers, who successfully ran the JOGS cinema circuit. By the early 1950s the Jewish population had started to move north into Moortown and Alwoodley and the cinema closed down in 1959 – with an appropriate film, *Salome*.

TELEPHONE—42755

FORUM CINEMA

CHAPELTOWN RD., LEEDS.

(No. 2 Tram from Briggate Barrier takes straight to Door).

BACK STALLS 3/9

(INCLUDING TAX)

"FOR WHOM THE BELL TOLLS."
EVENING at 6-30
Saturday, July 1st

This Ticket Reserves a Seat only at the Price Booked in that part of the Theatre and cannot be exchanged or cancelled under any circumstances

PLEASE RETAIN THIS PORTION

Above: *Interior of the Forum showing wall paintings and numerous radiators to heat the large hall.*

Left: *A booked ticket for a film show at the Forum in 1944.*

The Kingsway in its final days as a synagogue, prior to a fire and demolition.

Moortown

KINGSWAY (1937-1958)

The expanding West Leeds Amusements took over this cinema shortly before opening. It was built in 1937 but served the prosperous suburb of Moortown for only twenty-one. In September 1959 it reopened as the New Vilna synagogue. MP Gerald Kaufman was a regular worshipper and the funerals of both his parents were held here. The building was vacated in the 1980s and later burned down. The site was then fully cleared for use as flats.

Within a short distance, William Hobson, one time partner in West Leeds Amusements, opened his short-lived Corner House cinema eighteen months after the Kingsway, which he had built. The Corner House made a rule of not allowing admission if the feature had started. Previously on a continuous performance you could sometimes join the film in the middle and then leave when you reached the same point on the next run.

The cinema's other novelty was to have two newsreels, the Universal and G.B., 'Not to be found in any other cinema'.

These innovations by proprietor William Hobson hardly helped though, as the Corner House cinema was rapidly barred by the Kingsway and Forum and ceased operating after just eighteen months.

Roundhay

CLOCK (1938-1976)

Situated on a prominent position at a major junction, the Clock was a major investment for West Leeds Amusements and proved to be a sound business until the 1960s slump in attendances. Opening in 1938, it was the second cinema in the north of the city for the company. It seated over 1800 and for many decades was a popular venue. Sadly from the 1950s the city centre majors held films for longer and longer and the Clock was left with played-out titles. The end came in 1976 and attempts were made to lease out the cinema, but once again the mighty power of bingo prevailed. The Clock is now an electrical showroom.

Above: *The little-changed exterior of the Clock. After a period of bingo it was redeveloped as a retail store.*

Left: *Seats occupied by many people during the Clock's thirty-eight year cinema life.*

Harehills

PICTURE HOUSE (1912-1963)

The beautiful architecture of the marble entrance dome made the Picture House a local landmark. It was built by Harry Hylton's company and became the first in his eventual chain for Leeds & District Picture Houses Ltd. The Picture House seated 900 and opened with *The Mine Owner* in December 1912. Fireman 'Big' Jack commanded much respect from youngsters. For adults the entertainment included interludes from the five-piece orchestra led by Mr R. Millington. Even though the Clock opened in 1938 and was only minutes away, the Picture House remained open until 1963 when it became a bingo hall. It was demolished five years later to make way for shops and a supermarket.

HILLCREST (1920-1963)

Allan Nield, owner of the Malvern, made this his second cinema. He opened the Hillcrest in 1920 and included musical programmes from the popular orchestra of Bensley Ghent. The building also included a café where cinema bookings were taken. Closure came in 1963 and a replacement building has kept the Hillcrest name.

Take a bus to the bingo in Roundhay Road, formerly the site of the Picture House.

At the top of the hill the Hillcrest cinema lasted from 1920 to 1963.

The Gaiety cinema.

GAIETY (1921-1958)

When the Gaiety was demolished the statues were taken by *Coronation Street* actor Brian Mosley. He had grown up in the area and the statues graced his garden for many years. The ornate frontage of the cinema made it an instant attraction at the bottom of Roundhay Road. When it opened in 1921 it boasted a Saloon Orchestra under Philip Jacobs. Competition from TV and the nearby Clock cinema made the Gaiety an early closure in 1958.

York Road

VICTORIA (1912-1937)
This ornate picture house opened in 1912 and survived until it was demolished in 1937 to make way for the much more imposing Star.

SHAFTESBURY (1928-1975)
The Shaftesbury opened with a great attraction for couples – double seats. The cinema was also equipped with full stage facilities and alongside was a large ballroom, still operating as a club. The cinema was later taken over by ABC and in the late fifties stage shows were presented. Cliff Richard was one of the live attractions in 1959. The cinema closed for a short time to be a casino, but returned to film before final closure in 1975 with *Death Wish*. The façade of the cinema has been incorporated within an office complex.

The Victoria Picture House.

Take the tram and enjoy a picture at the Shaftesbury.

Above left: This frontage of the Shaftesbury is still preserved and the foyer is in use as a café.

Above right: Inside the projection box at the Shaftesbury.

STAR (1938-1961)

Goldstone Cinemas used land previously occupied by their Victoria cinema to build the impressive Star, which opened in 1938. Cinema shows ceased in 1961 when bingo took over. Today the old cinema is a gym and health club.

Newtown

NEWTOWN PICTURE PALACE (1913-1953)
Built in the heart of the first Jewish community, the Newtown in the Leylands specialised in Yiddish films, but once the immigrant population moved to the more affluent Chapeltown this cinema was left with a diminishing audience and closed in 1953.

Crossgates

PICTURE HOUSE (1920-1965)
This was the first cinema in the suburb and opened in 1920. In its heyday in the 1930s and '40s, Owen Brooks, the film pioneer, ended his distinguished career here as cinema manager. When

The Star cinema.

Left: The Newtown Picture Palace.

Below: The Picture House in Crossgates as the Ritz. Customers had the choice of hopping off the train and sampling the pub or pictures.

he looked back he could recall celluloid events as early as novelty movies at the Hippodrome Theatre. Always dedicated to the cinema, at the Picture House/Ritz during the Second World War Brooks even slept on the premises in case of an air raid. At the age of eighty-one in 1944, he still had the agility of a man thirty years his junior.

His two interests in life were novelty and speed – hence his passion for motorcycles as well as cinemas. When nineteen he took a grocer's shop in Dewsbury. A year later he decided to set part of the shop aside for a photographic studio.

After an American sold an Edison cine-projector to the Theatre Royal, Brooks studied the machine and realised that some original film had been shot too quickly and actors appeared to crawl across the screen. So, by means of a wringing machine wheel, he amended the gearing to make the characters more natural.

Around 1900 he decided to make his own film with one of the first cine cameras in the city. Across the streets of Leeds he shot travelogues from the top of trams and these were screened in between acts at the Hippodrome Theatre, Lands Lane.

Soon he was travelling further afield – first to Ireland for the Gordon Bennett motorcar races, and then to Hull to film damage done to trawlers by Russian gunboats. A real scoop was filming the arrival of the Black Prince statue being unloaded from a barge at Crown Point Bridge.

Brooks' other passion was motorbikes – he imported an engine from France and built his own, which was duly registered as U1 (cars and bikes shared the same number). U1 is still registered to the Mayor's car. Brooks' motorbike was a real speed king – once reaching 73mph.

During the war, in his more sedate years at the Ritz cinema, he raised £900 for the Red Cross. Owen Brooks died in 1947.

REGAL (1936-1964)

Its prominent position on the roundabout made the Regal more visible than the Picture House and its 1500 seats were regularly filled. Built in the dark days of the thirties it promised to 'beat the bogey of depression'. It took twenty-seven weeks to build in 1936, and just ten days to demolish in 1964. It was owned by the wireless and electrical firm Ainsley's, and was their sole cinema. Bob Hill started here as a projectionist in 1954 and went on to become the circuit engineer for the Odeon chain in the north. His foresight has given us valuable pictures of the two Odeons in Leeds – together with the final show at the Regal as the demolition crew clear the site for a new American-style shopping mall.

The Regal in Crossgates – opened in 1936.

0095

REGAL
CROSSGATES.
LEEDS.

1st

STALLS

ADMISSION 1/-
INCLUDING TAX

Row...................

No......................

Date..................

FIRST HOUSE

Left: *Inside the Regal projection box.*

Above: *A ticket for the Regal's opening show.*

Below: *With its advertising poster still intact, the Regal faces its Longest Day as the end approaches.*

Burmantofts

REGENT (1916-1971)

In this heavily populated area, the Regent was a beacon attracting thousands of customers who wished to escape their drab surroundings. The cinema was part of Leeds and District Picture Houses Ltd from its beginning and, although on an unmade up road, was always a popular hall.

A famous publicity stunt in the 1930s involved an aeroplane flying from the newly opened Leeds-Bradford airport to perform stunts over the Regent and then to dispense leaflets. For this reason for the cinema's name was painted on the roof – the pilot had difficulty identifying the cinema amongst the densely packed area.

Later through the fifties, housing clearances left the Regent with a diminished audience. Then a massive fire virtually destroyed the building, but with Louis Mannix's enthusiasm it reopened in 1963. To rejuvenate clientele, Mannix took on the self-imposed task of personally visiting every house in the area to introduce himself and make customers aware of the reopening. It then ran happily until the retirement of Louis Mannix in 1970. Sold to an amusement company, it continued as a cinema until May 1971 before turning to bingo.

The Regent in its bingo era. The roof name was painted to identify the cinema from the air.

Damage caused by the fire at the screen end of the Regent. Return of the Vampire *(X) was the final film before the fire on 16/1/60. The Regent reopened on 3/6/63 with the Elvis Presley feature* Girls, Girls, Girls.

After refurbishment the Regent enjoyed many years of solid business.

MALVERN (1912-1971)

This was Allan Nield's first cinema that he ran under the company name of Paragon Pictures Ltd. The Malvern opened in late 1912 and became a firm favourite with the people of Beeston. It merged with Leeds and District Picture Houses Ltd in the late 1950s and ran until this company was dissolved in 1970. Under Noble's Amusements it was a cinema until August 1971. The final manager was Tony Atkinson, who had started with Leeds and District as a projectionist at the Crown straight from school. He worked at all of their cinemas before being appointed manager of the Malvern, which he remembers as a truly wonderful time. Bingo was planned after the cinema's closure, but never materialised and the stylish building was demolished three years later.

1911 **MALVERN,** Beeston 1971. Special announcement to patrons! It is with regret that we must announce that after 60 years of Family Entertainment the Cinema must close its doors as such after the final performance on Saturday, August 28.

1911 **MALVERN, BEESTON,** 1971. The first "Carry On" film. "CARRY ON SERGEANT" (U) plus "CARRY ON TEACHER" (U). Cont. from 6.0. Last full show 7.30

Top: *The Malvern cinema on Beeston Road.*

Above: *The final shows at the Malvern.*

Right: *A poster advertising the Malvern.*

The Queen's – a former theatre that later turned to pictures.

Holbeck

QUEEN'S PICTURE THEATRE (1924-1957)

The Queen's Theatre in Jack Lane opened in 1898 and was converted for cinema use from December 1924. In the mid–1930s part of the building was used by the Yorkshire Television Association for experiments and discussions about the new medium.

The Queen's was a vast building and in the fifties was renowned for an unruly audience – so much so that an attendant with a long pole used to prod disruptive teenagers, who frequented this picture palace in large numbers.

Hunslet

ALHAMBRA, LOW ROAD (1912-1914)

The Alhambra was opened in 1912 by Herbert Pemberton, a man of immense energy and creativity. He produced a number of films, including *My Yorkshire Lass* in 1916, at the Pyramid Studios in Bradford. The following year his second was *Nearer My God to Thee* starring three national stars, Henry Edwards, Chrissie White and A.V. Bramble. What appears to have been his final film came in 1918, *Bonnie Mary*. Two other scripts have been found, *My English Rose* and *Come Back to Erin*, but it seems that neither of these were filmed. Happily the National Film Archive has copies of the brochures and sections of the scripts, but copies of the original films have yet to surface.

The Alhambra had a Moorish design inspired by the structure in Granada. An orchestra was a feature of the cinema and Pemberton was one of the players. In spite of the quality of the cinema it was a short-lived enterprise. A year after opening the cinema was converted back into its original purpose as a warehouse and at the same time Pemberton bought the German-owned Pavilion opposite.

The original Alhambra became a munitions factory during the war, and subsequently a snooker hall, dance hall and skating rink.

PAVILION (1913-1959)

Built a year after the Alhambra and just opposite was the Pavilion. It was owned by a consortium of German businessmen but once the war was imminent they were faced with either internment or deportation. They decided to sell up and go back to Germany. Pemberton took the opportunity to take over his competitor and the Pavilion became the premier hall in Hunslet – always previewing Pemberton's films before they were screened in the city centre. He ran this cinema until 1931 and the cinema continued as the Regal until 1959.

Many Hunslet residents remember with great affection this cinema where they went as youngsters for the Saturday afternoon show. At 4.00 p.m. all the kids would pour out still imagining they were still in the Wild West.

As the youngsters grew up they enjoyed their courting days at the Pavilion where most nights Mr Pemberton serenaded them with his violin, playing from a little balcony. Then the curtain opened and the big film began – all that romance for just 9d.

Above left: Jack Calvert, owner of the Regal garage, displays posters found in the old Pavilion building.

Above right: Two of the posters from the Pavilion.

Armley

WESTERN (1910-1956)

Converted from a chapel, Pictureland was opened in 1910 by the American Bioscope Company, but was taken over within three months by Charles Metcalfe and Tommy Thompson. It became the Western Talkie in 1933 and closed in 1956. Leslie Shann reopened it the following year and ran it as the New Western for three years. Today it's a café with bingo and amusements.

PALACE (1912-1956)

Not far away from the Western was the Palace, a conversion of the old Armley Rink (1910) which reopened as a cinema in August 1912. Seating 800 it was packed to capacity on its opening night and enjoyed a long life, finally succumbing to bingo in 1964.

The Western, so named from 1933 to 1956, in Branch Road, Armley

The old Western in its modern guise, still providing amusement in Armley.

LYRIC (1922-1988)

On opening day in 1922 no pictures were shown because the equipment wasn't fully installed, but a musical programme entertained patrons. This was the first cinema in what was to become a small chain for West Leeds Amusements Ltd. Although closing in 1976, a month before the company's Clock and Rex, the Lyric luckily found new operators. It reopened in November but only ran for six months before closing for another two years. John and Pat Kingston then lovingly restored the building and tried patiently to increase business during their nine-year tenure. Sadly it was forced to close through lack of custom in 1988.

Opposite: *The Crown, Wortley – on bingo from 1968.*

Left: *The final programme produced for the Lyric.*

Below: *The exterior of the Lyric.*

Wortley

CROWN (1919-1968)

This was the second Crown cinema in Wortley – the first, almost opposite, ran from 1911 to 1916, by which time building had begun on this new one. Wartime delays meant the new cinema didn't open until 1919, but once it did it became a popular hall in this packed part of Leeds. Its opening programme included a newsreel of the Grand National run just three days earlier. The Crown became the first suburban cinema in Leeds to be installed with Western Electric sound equipment and was part of the chain, Leeds and District Picture Houses Ltd.

Above and below: *Two interior shots of the Crown.*

The Lido cinema.

Bramley

LIDO (1912-1961)

The Bramley Picture House was William Hobson's first cinema, which he opened in 1912. It became the Lido in 1931 and was operated for many years by the Segelman family. Closure came in 1961 after a long battle for audiences with the nearby and more modern Clifton.

CLIFTON (1939-1961)

Tramlines passed the site of the Clifton at Town End in Bramley for many years, providing easy transport to Cansfield's third cinema in Leeds. Their Dominion had opened in 1934, followed three years later by the Savoy, Stanningley. This had been built in the garden of Lambert Cansfield's house, Westfield, in Bradford Road. The Savoy seated 950 and was modelled on the Dominion, again built of solid Yorkshire stone. Opening on Friday 17 September 1937, the new luxury Savoy cinema very quickly built up a loyal clientele and survived until 1965.

The Clifton cinema, the last of the trio, seated 1250, and was virtually identical to the Savoy. Coloured lighting on the Clifton made it an eye-catching site in the evening – the red and green neon and the floodlighting created a beacon for customers throughout its twenty-two year cinema life from January 1939 to June 1961. Within a few days of closure an auction was held for all the internal fixtures, including seats and projection equipment.

None of the Cansfield trio still exist. The Clifton was demolished in October 2001, the Dominion was replaced by housing in 2000 and the Savoy disappeared in 1998.

Top and above: *The Clifton cinema.*

Left: *The sad and final end of pictures at the Clifton.*

The Abbey Picture House.

Kirkstall

ABBEY (1913-1960)

This bijou picture palace, very near to the ancient Kirkstall Abbey, opened in 1913 and advertised itself with 400 tip-up and 120 upholstered seats. From an orchestral balcony a duo provided music with violin and piano. The cinema soldiered on until 1960 when bingo took over.

Burley

HADDON HALL (1914-1960)

A Tudor frontage once concealed this large cinema seating 737. It opened on Bankfield Terrace in 1914 and ran to 1960 before turning to bingo for many years. The picture house served a localised area and was not visible from any main road. In the mid-1970s enquiries were made about reopening the building as a cinema but were curtailed by objections from residents.

Above: *The exterior of the Lyceum as bingo hall just prior to demolition.*

Opposite above: *The Tudor frontage that once led to the Haddon Hall cinema.*

Opposite below: *The front of the Imperial cinema.*

IMPERIAL (1913-1940)

The building still stands in a much-changed Kirkstall Road. Once the area contained tightly packed streets and supported six local picture houses – the Burley Picture House, the Lyceum, the King's Lighthouse, the Haddon Hall, the Gem and the Imperial, which opened in 1913 and closed in 1940.

LYCEUM (1913-1968)

This family-run cinema opened in 1913 and was popular throughout its fifty-five-year history. Because of competition from the Lounge and Hyde Park it was only able to book Universal and United Artists pictures, but certainly held its own through constant updating and innovation. Like many others it found bingo provided a better income than pictures and closed as a cinema in 1968, two months before nearby Yorkshire Television opened. The cinema was finally demolished in April 1988.

Above and below: *In 1955 a cinemascope system was installed at the Lyceum. Here we see the narrow proscenium and then the vast new screen, improving the cinema experience and hopefully the profits.*

four

Out of town cinemas

Birstall

SHOWCASE (1989-PRESENT)

The Showcase used the same logic for its location as had Jimmy Corrigan when he built the Batley Variety Club in 1967. Within a few miles of here was a vast population and the opening of the Showcase changed cinema economics forever. The city centre cinemas in Leeds, Bradford, Huddersfield and Halifax all suffered after the opening of this Birstall multiplex in 1989.

The Showcase offered a fresh image for a new generation who had tired of the traditional and often outdated look of existing cinemas. Here neon lights, fast food and a luxury style attracted crowds from all over West Yorkshire. Within three years of opening, two extra screens were added.

However, the party was not to last. The Warners multiplex in Kirkstall stole back customers from Leeds and the Jacob's Well multiplex attracted many customers back to Bradford. The Odeon cinema at Thornbury also bites into audiences from Bradford and Leeds.

Once the Ster Century cinemas opened on the Headrow, Leeds, it is hard to assess the market share of each of the area's four multiplexes. In the last few years both the UCI at Crystal Peaks in Sheffield and the UCI at St Andrew's Quay in Hull have closed.

It's a tough business, as shown by the recent sale of most chains. The business evolves and there are winners and losers. It is twenty-five years since I first wrote *Leeds Cinemas Remembered*. If another book is published in twenty-five years time, how much more change will that report?

The answer is in your hands… happy cinema going!

The Birstall Showcase.

Garforth

Cinemas opened in the same year, 1913, in both Garforth and nearby Kippax. The Garforth Picture House ran until 1964 and closed with the James Bond blockbuster, *Thunderball*. The Alhambra in Kippax had gone to bingo in 1960, and their three evening sessions produced such good returns it subsidised the Garforth cinema for the next four years.

Horsforth

The imposing Glenroyal seated 900 and opened in November 1937, competing with Horsforth's original Imperial (1925-1960). After the Glenroyal closed in 1964 it was converted into a supermarket, which it remains today.

Left: *The Garforth Picture House.*

Below: *The former Glenroyal cinema in Horsforth.*

Palace Electric Pictures, Lowtown, Pudsey.

A rare photograph of the Temperance Hall, Rawdon.

Pudsey

The Palace Picture House at Lowtown in Pudsey ran for fifty years until closure for bingo in 1960. Pudsey's Picture House in Church Street also closed in the same year and was later converted into a supermarket.

Rawdon

The upstairs part of the old Temperance Hall was converted for cinema shows from 1925, but these were soon replaced by theatrical shows until the early 1930s when cinema came back to the fore. The Segelman circuit took over from 1940 to 1954 when they sold the lease to Robert Bassist, who struggled for less than two years before his bankruptcy spelled the end of pictures at the Rawdon Empire.

Stanningley

The Savoy was the second of the Cansfield circuit, opening in 1937, three years after the Dominion. Its solid Yorkshire stone remained a local landmark long after films ceased in 1965. It went to bingo until demolition in 1998.

The Royal bingo hall, formerly the Savoy cinema.

The Wetherby Film Theatre.

The interior of Studio 2 at Yeadon, seating 117.

Wetherby

The Wetherby cinema celebrated its ninetieth birthday in 2005. It opened originally to entertain troops stationed nearby during the First World War, and became a billet for soldiers shortly after opening. For many years it was powered entirely by a gas engine. It was taken over in the early 1950s by Star Cinemas and made a personal project for Walter Eckart's son Rodney. The Rodney cinema ran until 1964, after which bingo sessions were played. Even this venture failed in 1993 and the following July, after much refurbishment, the Wetherby Film Theatre reopened with *Four Weddings and a Funeral*. Today, very much part of the local community, it enjoys strong loyal support.

Yeadon

Yeadon's Picture House on the High Street was the fourth in the town when it opened in 1925. Other halls were the Gem Palace, Palace Pictures (in the Town Hall) and the Temperance Hall (1911-1963). The modern Picture House was twinned in the 1970s, becoming known as Studio 1 and 2.

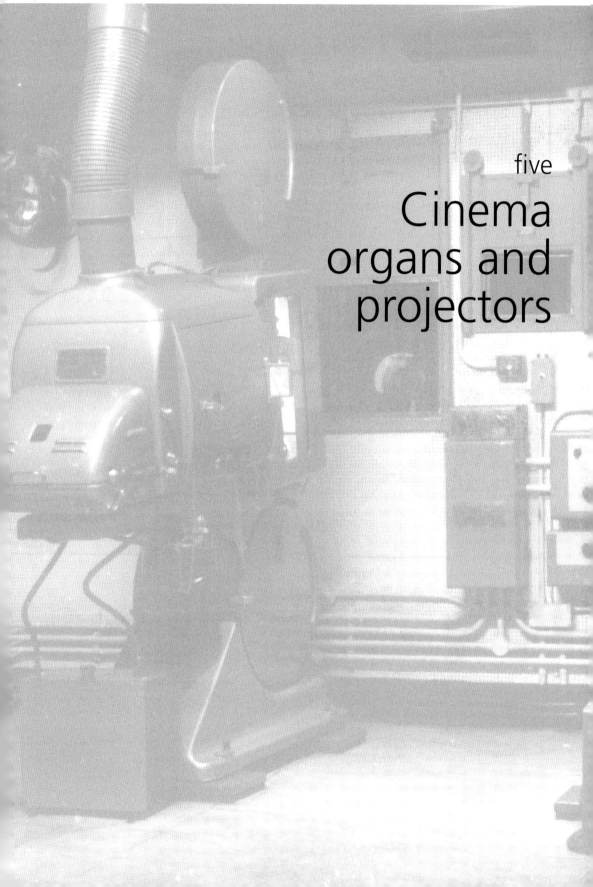

five

Cinema
organs and
projectors

Gifted pianists who accompanied the silent films paved the way for more sophisticated musicianship, recalls W. Iles Pulford.

'Some cinemas had real orchestras, notably the Lounge. There, complete with the Conacher organ, Fred Kitchen conducted some twenty players, using carefully selected music, properly rehearsed, with the organ as a link between styles.

'The New Gallery in South Parade had an orchestra under Bensley Ghent with a similar selection of appropriate music. The Coliseum had a very fine four manual organ high up in the proscenium arch upon which many distinguished recitalists performed between the pictures, while the pianist improvised during the film.

'And it was the gift of improvisation that mattered. The pianists, often hidden by a dusty curtain at an angle to the screen, matched their music to the picture. Most organists also improvised to swap rapidly between moods – from anxious to terror then into relief – all within seconds.

'When I accompanied Ben Hur at a cinema in London, I very quickly learnt the art. We had chariot races, murders and mayhem, followed shortly by romance. All this had to be in the right key. C major is very unromantic – all these scenes had to be in F sharp major. We played unrehearsed pieces night after night – and the aching fingers only stopped after a hurried tribute to royalty.

'Today we see magnificent pictures and excellent acting, but why do we have to hear a full symphony orchestra playing behind a couple like Bing and Grace in a small boat. Was it really television that killed cinema? Give me radio anytime!'

By the early 1950s the cinema organ was redundant. The Odeon Wurlitzer was only used for Sunday concerts and special occasions – with the Ritz the only one in regular use.

1954 was a decisive year, with four cinema organs removed. A Leeds man, Mr W. Dickinson, had set up an organ repair business in Truro and was given the task of dismantling the organs at the Scala, the Majestic, Lounge and Crown. One manager explained, 'We have no use for them these days. Our type of programme is the quick, get-on-with-it entertainment.' Another said that in the past patrons could enjoy good performances, but these days there are too many mediocre players. All four organs were to be modernised and reused in churches, mainly in South Wales.

LOUNGE
Conacher straight three manual organ installed in 1919. Removed in 1954.

COLISEUM
Original pipe organ replaced in 1920 by a four manual Abbott & Smith machine.

CRESCENT
Single manual Brindley & Foster 'Clavorchestra', installed in 1921 at a cost of £3,000. Removed in 1954.

MAJESTIC
Costing £5,000, the three manual Vincent organ was opened by Harry Davison in 1922. This was rebuilt in the 1930s as a fifteen-unit model and removed in 1954.

LYRIC
1922 Fitton organ, scrapped in 1952 when the cinemascope screen was installed.

CROWN

The Crown had an organ in the mid-1920s, which was removed in 1954.

PICTURE HOUSE, BEESTON

From 1927 this cinema had a two manual Wood & Wordsworth organ.

BEESTON
PICTURE HOUSE.

" The Mecca of the Music Lover."

———— 'Phone 27120. ————

Managing Director :

L. DENHAM.

Resident Manager :

L. J. MANNIX.

GRAND OPENING

OF THE

MIGHTY
ORCHESTRAL
ORGAN

ON

Friday, 30th September, 1927,

BY

Ald. HARRY BRIGGS

Chairman   - ·   Councillor G. BRETT.

At the Organ   -   -   -   **ALBAN CHAMBERS, Mus. Bac., F.R.C.O., A.R.C M.**

Orchestra under the direction of   -   -   -   -   **F. CHIODINI (Director of Music)**

Vocal Items by   -   -   -   -   -   -   -   -   **WM. NUTTER (Baritone)**

ONE PERFORMANCE ONLY.

Doors Open   -   7-0 p.m.   Patrons are respectfully requested to

Commence   -   7-30 p.m.   be in their seats at 7-30 prompt.

Advance Booking :   NO EXTRA CHARGE.

The programme advertising the opening of the organ at the Beeston Picture House.

Rex O'Grady played the first notes on the Paramount Wurlitzer. The organ was removed prior to twinning and is preserved at the Thursford Steam Museum in Norfolk.

SCALA
Compton two manual six-unit organ installed in 1930. Removed in 1954.

PARAMOUNT
£20,000 three manual ten-unit installed in 1932 and played from opening by Rex O'Grady. Removed in 1968 during the twinning of the Odeon.

RITZ
1934 Compton three manual ten-unit. Removed in 1968 during twinning and preserved in Leicestershire.

FORUM
The Forum had a 1936 Lafleur/Hammond electronic organ. This was replaced in 1946 by a Christie two manual five-unit organ, but this was broken up when the cinema closed in 1959.

Leeds was also home to one of the major projector manufacturers. Abram Kershaw came from Bradford but was firmly against going into the woollen mills. After a move to Leeds he began making scientific instruments for the army. His son then took a great interest in engineering and together they set up a factory making cinema equipment for Sydney Carter. The first Kalee projector was turned out in 1911 and six years later the company moved to a new factory in Harehills Lane.

From this base they built up a huge concern supplying projectors and in the 1950s added lenses to the trade. Abram Kershaw died in 1929 but his work was continued by his family and eventually became part of the Rank Organisation.

The Harehills Lane factory, which made projectors from 1910 to 1958, had once employed 3,000 people. It closed in 1980 but even today over 4,000 Kalee projectors still operate throughout the world. Spare parts are now manufactured in Japan.

The Kalee projector at the Plaza in Leeds ran from 1954 until 1985 and never failed once – in spite of all those steamy pictures it showed.

The Plaza projection room, showing the long-serving Kalee.

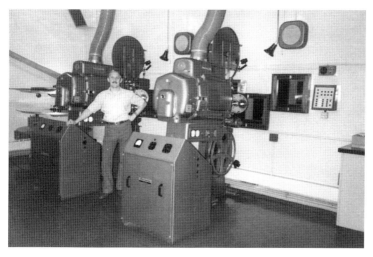

Bob Hill in the Odeon 2 projection box.

Above left: *The projector used for the 'Screen In the Square' festival, May 1981, in the former Classic cinema.*

Above right: *The Lounge, 1981.*

Left: *Odeon, Merrion Centre, 1977.*

Left: *Cottage Road, 1981.*

Below: *John Kingston at the Lyric, Tong Road, 1981.*

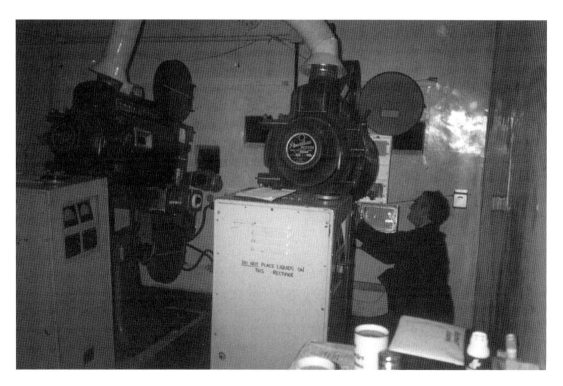

Lyceum, Cardigan Road.

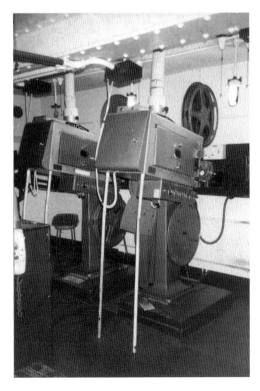

Left: *Tower Cinema, Briggate.*

Opposite above: *Playhouse Film Theatre.*

Opposite below: *Majestic, City Square.*

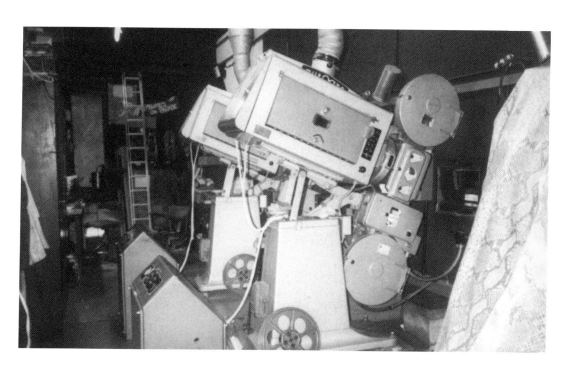

Hyde Park, 1980.

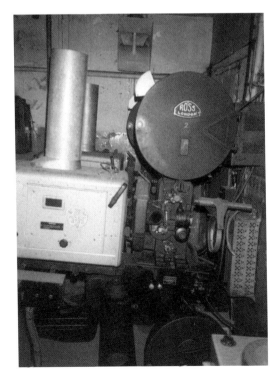

Ritz, Woodlesford, 1971.

six

Cinema
chains and
entrepreneurs

Many cinema owners ran just one screen, but the lure of a chain was never far from their minds. Although there are few scales of economy, a cinema chain could increase the owner's film booking power. It also helped to see off unwanted competition from other entrepreneurs.

In Leeds there was a significant Jewish presence amongst cinema operators. Perhaps encouraged by the big Hollywood names like the Warner brothers, Louis B. Mayer, Harry Cohn, Sam Goldwyn, and in Britain, Michael Balcon local businessmen quickly saw the popularity of films and cinemas.

At the bottom of Chapeltown Road, once the heart of Leeds Jewry, was the Forum cinema – owned by Simon Newman and operated by Gerald Segelman until 1950, when he handed the lease to his brothers.

Gerald's father, Max, had initially taken the Alexandra Picture House in Camp Road, Woodhouse in 1924. Later his four sons Jack, Oscar, Gerald, and Sydney formed the JOGS circuit controlling twenty northern cinemas. Jack Segelman, who personally owned nine cinemas from Harrogate down to Doncaster, was renowned as a shrewd film booker, well able to hold his own against the tough distributors along Wellington Street – the Leeds version of Wardour Street.

In 1940 the JOGS circuit took over the lease at the Rawdon Empire. This cinema had a chequered history of operators, but the Segelmans proved their expertise and ran it successfully before selling the lease in 1954 – wisely sensing the beginning of the end. The Empire finally closed within two years. Jack Segelman retired to Devon while Sydney was also drawn to the coast when he purchased the Palace cinema in St Anne's. Ten years later, in 1964, he sold this to Eckart's Star circuit, also based in Leeds.

The humble beginnings of the Star group came in 1931 with the purchase of the Star Palace in Castleford. By 1950 Walter Eckart, a former toy importer, had slowly built a sizeable circuit of 124 cinemas. This peaked nine years later with 180 cinemas, mostly in the north, but including twenty-seven in London. The sixties saw the group diversify into skating rinks, bingo and nightclubs. And from the late 1950s to the mid-1960s the Star Cinema Film Unit, based in Leeds, produced numerous two-reel shorts for showing at their own cinemas and also to be distributed nationwide by Anglo-Amalgamated. Walter Eckart died in 1964 and his two sons spent a decade at the helm in possibly the group's most prosperous period. However, by the mid-1970s tax evasion and financial irregularities led the brothers to a year's imprisonment in Armley jail. Their bingo chain was sold for £5.7 million to EMI, who had previously held a 50 per cent share in a third of the Star bingo halls.

Smaller operators in Leeds included Sam Freeman and Jacob Bickler at the Palladium Picture Palace in Holbeck's Sweet Street, while in Roundhay, the Managing Director of the Gaiety was Barnet Caverson.

Jewish entrepreneurs Morris Cohen and Herman White ran not only the Picture House in Easy Road but also the nearby Princess at Richmond Hill. They later opened the Strand cinema in Jack Lane. Morris Goodman opened the Grosvenor on Camp Road, while Reuben Churnin ran the adjacent Victory. Over in Hunslet Carr, Gerry Fontheim ran the Leasowe Picture Palace from 1911 to 1916, while Rodley's Picture House in Town Street was successful in its early days from 1927 under Mark Morris.

Goldstone Cinemas Ltd was an enterprising company that expanded in the thirties. From 1920 Max Goldstone had the Wellington, and in 1930 he took over the Pavilion, installed sound and renamed it the Regal, Hunslet. The company opened Middleton's new Tivoli in 1934 and their Victoria Picture Palace was replaced in 1938 by their largest cinema, the Star – still standing in York Road.

Top: *Rodley's Picture House, shown in 1970. It bears the name of the Rialto, but was by then a factory.*

Above left: *The Wellington Picture House, Max Goldstone's first venture into the cinema business.*

Above right: *The Palace on Meadow Road, Holbeck.*

The Tower group of cinemas in March 1940.

Jewish designers also played a major role in cinema architecture. A.V. Montague planned the Regal, Cross Gates and the Rex, Beeston while the 1960s Odeon Merrion Centre was designed by Messrs Gillinson and Barnett.

Other notable circuits in the city were the Walker family's West Leeds Amusements, whose halls included the Lyric, Clock and the Rex; Cansfield's Westfield Pictures Ltd ran three massive suburban cinemas, the Dominion in Chapel Allerton, the Clifton in Bramley and the Savoy in Stanningley from the late 1930s to the late '60s. Jack Lambert of Harrogate ran Uni-Cinemas with offices in Mill Hill and halls in Bradford (Wyke), Rodley, Kippax and Garforth. The Lambert circuit also ran Wellington Film Distributors and operated the Rialto, Briggate from 1927 to closure twelve years later.

Two long-running cinema companies were formed in 1920. One was Leeds and District Picture Houses Ltd. Without access to company records, it is difficult to trace the development of the company but from existing documents it becomes possible to offer at least an outline.

Builder and contractor Harry Hylton had major financial interests in the Harehills Picture House (1912), Burley Picture House (1913), Morley Picture House (1913) and the Regent (1916). He may have built the Crown in Wortley in 1916, which was completed after the First World War to open in 1919. Certainly, together with Leonard Denham (manager of the Walturdaw Cinema Supplies Company in Leeds) he took over the Lounge in 1918.

Leeds and District Picture Houses Ltd (with directors Harry Hylton, Leonard Denham, Horace Boot and Miles and William Read) was formed in 1920 to purchase and take over from 7 June 1920 the North Lane Picture Lounge (at a cost of £70,000), the Crown on Tong Road (£41,000), the Regent on Torre Road (£34,000) and the newly opened Beeston Picture House (£10,000).

A separate company, Leeds Picture Playhouses Ltd, was formed to build the Majestic in 1921 and after opening Leonard Denham was its General Manager – and at the same time also managed the Lounge.

The Palace in Holbeck was taken over in 1932 and Beeston's Malvern was added in the 1950s. The company continued successfully until 1970, when Louis Mannix retired and the other directors, Gerald, Alfred and Richard Hylton decided the time was right to sell the assets of the company.

Also formed from 1920 was Associated Tower Cinemas. It began when the Tower in Briggate opened and brought together other Tower cinemas in York, Grimsby, Goole and Hull. Later the chain took over the Carlton in Leeds and made steady cinema and property acquisitions through the next few decades, including in 1930 the Pavilion in Stanningley, the Capitol (1934), Cottage Road (1938), Crescent (1944) and also during the Second World War the Palladium and Opera House in Ripon. The company diversified in 1957 with the purchase of the Astoria Ballroom and took over the Lounge cinema in 1970. More recently an associated company has built up a successful chain of bars and restaurants.

seven

Live shows at
the Odeon

Although Cliff Richard, the star of *Oh Boy!*, appeared live at the Shaftesbury cinema on York Road on 19 January 1959, it was to be the Odeon shows that will be forever remembered (not forgetting of course the all-star shows at the Empire – but then that's another book in itself).

For just eleven years the Odeon's big screen was occasionally hoisted away to allow top stars to bring their show to the city. From rock and roll to smooth jazz, it was a veritable feast for music fans as the world's top artists played for one night at the Odeon. Some shows even lasted a full week, so you're sure to recall your favourites from this list, published for the first time.

The Odeon, Leeds – The stage show era, 1957-1968

1957

14 February – Bill Haley and the Comets
19 April – The Platters

1958

20-25 January – The London Festival Ballet
30 January – The Glenn Miller Orchestra
19 April – Johnny Ray
14 May – Jazz at the Phil
18-24 May – Jackie Dennis Show
10 June – The Treniers
19 June – Victor Borge
22 September – The Hi-Lo's
13-18 October – Jazz Festival
2 November – Paul Robeson

1959

3 March – Louis Armstrong
11 April – Woody Herman
7 May – Jazz at the Phil
2 July – The Cliff Richard Show

1960

12 February – Adam Faith
6 April – Bobby Darin
19 April – The Everly Brothers
16 October – Judy Garland

1961

28 January – Dave Brubeck Quartet

15 May – Ella Fitzgerald
20-25 November – London Festival Ballet
29 November – Nina and Frederick

1962

11 April – Count Basie and his Orchestra
22 April – Frankie Vaughan / Tommy Trinder
10 May – Louis Armstrong and the All Stars
2 June – Shirley Bassey and the Nelson Riddle Orchestra
12 September – Chubby Checker / The Brook Brothers
3 October – Sarah Vaughan and George Shearing
19 October – The Everly Brothers and Frank Ifield
1 November – Sophie Tucker and Johnny Dankworth
23 November – The Dave Brubeck Quartet
28 November – Johnny Mathis / Ted Heath & His Music

1963

27 February – Ella Fitzgerald & Oscar Peterson Trio
22 March – Cliff Richard and the Shadows
7 April – Ken Dodd and Adam Faith
14 May – Sammy Davis Jnr
5 June – The Beatles / Roy Orbison
18 July – Nat King Cole & Ted Heath and His Music

3 October – Roy Orbison / Freddie and the Dreamers
18 October – Gerry and the Pacemakers / The Bachelors
25 October – Brook Benton / Timi Yuro / Dion
3 November – The Beatles
18 November – Stan Kenton & his Orchestra
27 November – Duane Eddy / Gene Vincent / The Shirelles
14 December – Helen Shapiro

1964

25 January – Tommy Dorsey Orch and Frank Sinatra Jnr
28 February – Duke Ellington & His Orchestra
11 March – The Searchers / Dusty Springfield
5 April – Ella Fitzgerald
12 May – Roy Orbison / Freddie and the Dreamers
1 October – The Hollies / Freddie and the Dreamers
22 October – The Beatles
4 November – Dionne Warwick / The Isley brothers
25 November – Dusty Springfield / Herman's Hermits

1965

4-9 January – 'Gerry's Xmas Cracker' featuring Gerry and the Pacemakers, The Hollies, The Fourmost, Danny Williams
26 January – Chuck Berry / Long John Baldry
24 February – Duke Ellington & His Orchestra
2 March – Roy Orbison / The Rockin Berries
19 March – Del Shannon / Herman's Hermits
25 March – The Supremes / Stevie Wonder / Georgie Fame
12 April – Ella Fitzgerald & Oscar Peterson Trio

26 April-1 May – The Red Navy
2 May – The Bachelors / Freddie Davis
15 May – Shirley Bassey / Cyril Stapleton Orchestra
22 May – The Hollies / The Walker Brothers
9 October – The Rolling Stones
15 October – The Everly Brothers / Cilla Black
4 November – Herman's Hermits / Billy Fury
11 November – Cliff Richard and the Shadows
21 November – Gene Pitney / Lulu & The Luvvers
2 December – Dizzy Gillespie & Jimmy Smith Trio

1966

18 February – Ella Fitzgerald & Duke Ellington
3 April – Roy Orbison
17 August – The Small Faces / Dave Berry
24 September – The Rolling Stones
9 October – The Walker Brothers / The Troggs
22 October – Georgie Fame / Eric Burdon and the Animals
4 November – The Hollies / The Small Faces
10 November – The Beach Boys / Lulu

1967

30 January – The Four Tops / Madeline Bell
5 March – Gene Pitney / The Troggs
15 March – The Hollies
23 March – Roy Orbison / The Small Faces
5 April – The Walker Brothers / Engelbert Humperdinck
14 May – Tony Bennet & the Count Basie Orchestra
23 June – Victor Borge
8 November – Engelbert Humperdinck / The Rockin Berries
15 November – Tom Jones / Kathy Kirby / Ted Heath Orchestra
12 December – Joan Baez

1968

1 March – Manitas de Plata
4 March – The Dubliners
20 March – Tony Bennet & Buddy Rich Orchestra
12 April – Gene Pitney / Status Quo
24 April – Count Basie & His Orchestra
9 May – Clancy Brothers & Tommy Meakem
15 May – Herman's Hermits / Dave Berry
24 June – Esther & Abi Ofarim

Live shows ceased when the Odeon closed for twinning.

The top stars over the eleven years:
1st equal – (5 shows each) Ella Fitzgerald / Roy Orbison
2nd – (4 shows) Herman's Hermits
3rd equal – (3 shows each) The Beatles / Cliff Richard / Everly Brothers / The Hollies

eight

Leeds cinemas – the reel roll-call

Those we have loved. Our favourite picture palaces. Their final name is given first.

ABBEY, Kirkstall Road
520 seats
Opens 22/09/13 – First film *The Web*
Closes 08/10/60 – Last film *Idle on Parade*

ABC (from 23/05/59); RITZ, Vicar Lane
1950 Seats
Opens 19/11/34 – *Those were the Days*
Twinned from 05/04/70
Tripled from 17/03/74
Closes 17/02/2000 – *American Beauty, Double Jeopardy, Shaheed Uddham Singh*

ALEXANDRA PICTURE THEATRE, Camp Road
402 seats
30/09/12 – *The Sphinx*
09/04/38 – *Counsel for Crime*

ALHAMBRA, Low Road, Hunslet
690 seats
Opens 07/04/13 – *Life of Christ*
Closes 15/10/14 – No film details advertised

ASTRA; PICTURE PALACE, Woodhouse Street
610 seats
01/11/11 – *Trafalgar*
02/08/58 – *Woman in a Dressing Gown*

CAPITOL, Green Road, Meanwood
1294 seats
27/11/22 – *The Prodigal Judge*
27/07/68 – *Bonnie and Clyde*

CARLTON CINEMA, Carlton Street, Little London
832 seats
29/03/20 – *A Tale of Two Cities*
03/04/65 – *Every Day's a Holiday*

CARR CROFT CINEMA, Carr Crofts, Armley
305 seats
31/05/12 – *The VC Hero*
17/10/31 – *Kissing Cup's Race*

CLASSIC; TATLER; NEWS THEATRE, City Square
290 seats
22/08/38 – Cartoons and news items including Popeye and Radio Parade
31/01/81 – *Sex Life in a Convent*
16/05/81 – Reopens as the 'Screen in the Square' for two-week festival of art films.
30/05/81 – Final film *Romeo and Juliet*

CLIFTON CINEMA, Stanningley Road, Bramley
1300 seats
30/01/39 – *Woman Against Woman*
17/06/61 – *Carry On Regardless*

CLOCK CINEMA, Easterly Road, Roundhay
1836 seats
21/11/38 – *The Hurricane*
28/02/76 – *Incredible Journey*

CORNER HOUSE CINEMA, Moortown
380 seats
28/11/38 – *A Yank at Oxford*
06/01/40 – No film details advertised

COSY (from 19/2/32); MINERS, York Road
450 seats
18/07/10 – licence granted
02/04/38 – *Dark Journey*

COTTAGE ROAD; HEADINGLEY PICTURE HOUSE, Cottage Road
590 seats
29/07/12 – 'Continuous performances from 6.00 p.m.'
1938 – Taken over by Associated Tower cinemas.
28/7/05 – *Madagascar.*
Scheduled for closure, but deserves to be saved.

CRESCENT, Dewsbury Road
1158 seats
01/08/21 – *Build Thy House*
13/07/68 – *The Man Outside*

WITH THE COMPLIMENTS OF
ASSOCIATED TOWER CINEMAS LTD.

The
CAPITOL

Cinema,
Cafe
and
Ballroom
MEANWOOD

PROGRAMME FOR MAY

It's capital at the Capitol!

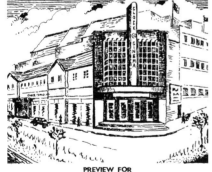

CLOCK CINEMA
HAREHILLS
Telephone: LEEDS 657341

PREVIEW FOR
FEBRUARY
PROGRAMMES SUBJECT TO ALTERATION

Top right: *The Crescent, after its conversion to bingo.*

Others: *Various cinema programmes from the 1940s, '50s and '60s.*

WITH THE COMPLIMENTS OF
Associated TOWER CINEMAS *Limited*

The
CARLTON
Cinema

CARLTON HILL
LEEDS

PHONE: 27279

MANAGER - - V. L. WINTERBURN

FOR YOUR INFORMATION

PRICES OF ADMISSION:
Circle 1/- (incl. 2½d. Tax and Levy)
Stalls 10d. (incl. 1½d. Tax and Levy)
Children under 14 — 10d.

APPROXIMATE TIMES OF
PERFORMANCES
Monday to Friday Cont. 6.15 – 10.30
Saturdays & Holidays Cont. 4.0 – 10.30
Sunday Two Distinct Performances
at 4.30 & 7.10
(All seats bookable in advance)

The Management reserve the right to alter
the advertised programme

"LET'S GO TO THE PICTURES"

Attractions for August, 1952

HEADINGLEY
PICTURE HOUSE
COTTAGE ROAD
LEEDS.6
TEL. 51606

CONTINUOUS PERFORMANCE FROM
6-10 APPROX EXCEPTING WEDNESDAYS
SATURDAYS & HOLIDAYS TWO DISTINCT
HOUSES AT 5-50 APPROX & 8-15

PROGRAMME
DECEMBER 1949 AND JANUARY 1950

ONE OF THE ASSOCIATED TOWER CINEMAS

WITH THE COMPLIMENTS OF
Associated TOWER CINEMAS *Limited*

The
CRESCENT
Cinema

DEWSBURY ROAD, LEEDS
Telephone 75747

'LET'S GO TO THE PICTURES'
ATTRACTIONS FOR JANUARY, 1952

CROWN CINEMA, Tong Road,
Wortley
899 seats
31/03/19 – *Over The Top*
21/09/68 – *Carry On Doctor* plus *The Plank*

CROWN ELECTRIC, Oldfield Lane,
Wortley
636 seats
18/09/11 – *The Cowboy's Deliverance*
16/09/16 – No closing details advertised

DEWSBURY ROAD PICTURE HALL,
Alpha Street, Beeston
433 seats
10/02/11 – 'The World's Best Pictures'
16/03/23 – No film details advertised

DOMINION CINEMA, Montreal
Avenue, Chapel Allerton
1486 seats
04/01/34 – *Cleaning Up*
18/03/67 – *The Quiller Memorandum*

EAST END PICTURE HALL, Places
Road, Richmond Hill
165 seats (former Mission Hall)
18/09/11 – Licence granted
Closed during First World War

ELECTRA PICTURE LOUNGE. Jubilee
Terrace, Woodhouse
660 seats (former church)
09/11/16 Licence granted
09/03/57 *Private's Progress*

EMBASSY (from 31/07/35); ATLAS,
Kirkstall Road
806 seats
01/05/12 – Licence granted
17/11/56 – *The Benny Goodman Story*

FORUM, Chapeltown Road,
Chapeltown
1500 seats
26/10/36 – *Colleen*
24/12/59 – *Salome*

GAIETY KINEMA, Roundhay Road
1046 seats
06/07/21 – *Carnival*- 'The film of the
century'
22/02/58 – *Woman in a Dressing Gown*

GAINSBOROUGH PICTURE HOUSE,
Domestic Street, Holbeck
578 seats (converted from chapel in 1927)
04/02/31 – Cinema Licence granted
22/10/66 – *Love For Sale*

GAUMONT-COLISEUM (from
24/10/38), COLISEUM, Cookridge Street
3000 seats, later reduced to 1700
17/04/1905 – New Century Pictures
including *A Holiday in Paris*
23/12/61 – *The Pied Piper of Hamblin*

GEM PICTURE HALL, Willoughby
Crescent, Holbeck
355 seats
26/10/12 – Licence granted
16/12/16 – No film details advertised

GOLDEN CROSS ELECTRIC
THEATRE, Meanwood Road
310 seats
24/12/10 – Licence granted
05/10/25 – No film details advertised

GROSVENOR PICTURE THEATRE,
Camp Road, Woodhouse
402 seats
19/12/12 – Licence granted
05/04/24 – No film details advertised

HADDON HALL PICTURE PALACE,
Bankfield Terrace, Burley
737 seats
16/02/14 – *The Fisher Girl of Venice*
30/07/60 – *Big Circus*

HILLCREST PICTURE LOUNGE,
Harehills Lane, Harehills
1131 seats
31/12/20 – *The Woman Thou Gavest Me*
09/11/63 – *Courage of Black Beauty*

HILLCREST
PICTURE LOUNGE

General Manager .... M. L. COLLINS

PROGRAMME SUBJECT TO ALTERATION

MONDAY to SATURDAY

Continuous from 5.45 p.m.

Sunday continuous 5.0

Telephone 27691   May, 1961

PRESENTED WITH THE COMPLIMENTS OF

THE LYCEUM CINEMA
Cardigan Road, Leeds 6

Manager: JOHN R. BROADLEY.   Tel. 5 1 7 6 5

Prices of Admission - - - - - 1/- and 1/6

Seats Bookable for Saturdays

(Booking Plans open every evening, 6-0 to 9 p.m.
— and Saturdays, 10 a.m. to 12 noon) ——

Continuous Performance Monday - Friday from approx. 6-0
Two Separate Houses Saturdays at 6-0 and 8-30 p.m.
These Programmes are subject to alteration without notice.

Keep this Programme handy as all members of the family
will want to refer to it.

Programme for MAY, 1957

MOVIES ARE **STILL** THE FINEST ENTERTAINMENT.

Above and left: *Three cinema programmes, including one from the Lyceum, defending movies as being 'still the best entertainment'.*

Below: *An advert promoting visits to the cinema.*

HYDE PARK PICTURE HOUSE (Leeds) **LTD.**

HYDE PARK
◆
PICTURE HOUSE

Phone: 52045

BRUDENELL ROAD   LEEDS 6

Secretary
A. J. CHILD

Manager
F. TAYLOR

PROGRAMME FOR SEPTEMBER

Monday to Friday ——— Continuous from 6-15

Saturdays and Holidays — 6-15 and 8-30 (approx.)

Let's go to the **pictures**

Issued by

ASSOCIATED BRITISH FILM DISTRIBUTORS LTD
ASSOCIATED BRITISH PATHE LTD
BRITISH LION FILM CORPORATION LTD
BUTCHERS FILM SERVICE LTD
COLUMBIA PICTURES CORPORATION LTD
EROS FILMS LTD
EXCLUSIVE FILMS LTD
GENERAL FILM DISTRIBUTORS LTD
INDEPENDENT FILM DISTRIBUTORS LTD
INTERNATIONAL FILM DISTRIBUTORS LTD
METRO-GOLDWYN-MAYER PICTURES LTD
NATIONAL SCREEN SERVICE LTD
PARAMOUNT FILM SERVICE LTD
RENOWN PICTURES CORPORATION LTD
REPUBLIC PICTURES INTERNATIONAL INC
RKO RADIO PICTURES LTD
TWENTIETH CENTURY-FOX FILM CO LTD
UNITED ARTISTS CORPORATION LTD
WARNER BROTHERS PICTURES LTD

THE CINEMA
provides all family entertainment
at a moderate price with every regard for your
comfort. It has become part of our lives; of our
conversation. Week by week the world's best stories,
factual and fictional—adventure, drama, comedy—
are brought to the screen with increasing skill
and imagination. All great actors and actresses
of the world lend their full talents to films.

There is no finer entertainment
at any price, anywhere

Members of the

KINEMATOGRAPH RENTERS' SOCIETY LIMITED

HUNSLET PICTURE HALL,
Hulland Road
590 seats
23/05/11 – Licence granted
1918 – No film details advertised

HYDE PARK PICTURE HOUSE,
Brudenell Road, Headingley
587 seats
07/11/14 – *Their Only Son*
Remains open under council ownership

IMPERIAL PICTURE HOUSE,
Kirkstall Road
700 seats
01/09/13 – Licence granted
22/5/40 – *The Girl from Mexico*

KING'S LIGHTHOUSE, North Hall Street,
Kirkstall
416 seats
15/04/11 – Licence granted
31/12/15 – No film details advertised

KING'S PICTURE THEATRE, Holbeck
Lane, Holbeck
800 seats
22/09/11 – *What Happened to Mary*
03/04/25 – No film details advertised

KINGSWAY, Harrogate Road,
Moortown
1150 seats
28/06/37 – *Head Over Heels*
23/08/58 – *Sayonara*

LEASOWE PICTURE PALACE,
Hunslet Carr, Hunslet
390 seats
23/12/10 – Licence granted
23/12/17 – No film details advertised

LIDO (from 06/05/31); PICTURE
PALACE, Lower Town Street, Bramley
520 seats
05/09/12 – Licence granted
08/03/61 – *The Nudist Story*

LOUNGE, Headingley
782 seats
02/10/1916 – *Cynthia In The Wilderness*
06/01/2005 – *Phantom of the Opera*

LYCEUM PICTURE HOUSE, Cardigan
Road, Burley
708 seats
07/05/13 – No film details advertised
11/05/68 – *Guess Who's Coming to Dinner*

LYRIC PICTURE HOUSE, Tong Road,
Armley
900 seats
09/12/22 – *The Three Musketeers*
03/01/76 – *Trap on Cougar Mountain*
Reopens
08/01/76 – *Shout at the Devil*
Closes
30/05/77 – *The Seventh Voyage of Sinbad*
Reopens
10/12/79 – *Star Wars*
Final closure
01/12/88 – *Good Morning Vietnam*

MAJESTIC, City Square
2500 seats
05/06/22 – *Way Down East*
10/07/69 – *The Good, the Bad and the Ugly*

MALVERN PICTURE PALACE, Beeston
Road, Beeston
850 seats
23/12/12 – *A Girl's Bravery*
28/08/71 – *Carry On Sergeant* and *Carry On Teacher*

MANOR PICTURE HOUSE, Manor
Road, Holbeck
540 seats
03/01/16 – No film details advertised
28/06/37 – *Enemies of The Public*

NEW GALLERY KINEMA,
South Parade
850 seats
22/03/20 – *Intolerance*
10/06/22 – *A Master Stroke*

NEW PALLADIUM; PICTURE HOUSE, Easy Road, Cross Green
699 seats
30/10/11 – *The White Chief*
15/03/59 – *What Price Glory*

NEWTOWN PICTURE PALACE, Cross Stamford Street, Sheepscar
788 seats
11/01/13 – *A Cruel Fate*
02/09/53 – *Captain Blood, Fugitive*

NEW WESTERN; WESTERN TALKIE; PICTURELAND, Branch Road, Armley
439 seats
25/04/10 – No film details advertised
30/12/60 – *The Unforgiven*

ODEON (from 15/04/40); PARAMOUNT THEATRE, The Headrow
2590 seats
22/02/32 – *The Smiling Lieutenant*
Twinned from 15/05/69
Odeon 3 opened in old bar 23/07/78
Screens 4 and 5 opened 01/04/88

28/10/2001 – Final films – *Jeepers Creepers, American Pie 2, Atlantis, American Sweethearts, The Fast and the Furious, Cats and Dogs*

ODEON, Merrion Centre
900 seats
17/08/64 – *The Fall of the Roman Empire*
01/10/77 – *Gone with the Wind*

OLYMPIA PICTURE HALL, Cherry Row, Mabgate
390 seats
02/09/12 – No film details advertised
16/03/34 – No film details advertised

PALACE, Westfield Road, Burley
308 seats
10/03/13 – No film details advertised
03/03/16 – No film details advertised

PALACE; PEOPLE'S PICTURE PALACE, Meadow Road, Holbeck
1077 seats
22/01/15 – No film details advertised
03/06/61 – *Back to God's Country*

Left and above: *Two 1950s programmes from the Palace in Armley.*

PALACE PICTURE HALL, Eyres Avenue,
Armley
800 Seats
26/08/12 – *The Governor's Daughter*
22/08/64 – *Summer Magic*

PALLADIUM PICTURE PALACE, Bridge
Road, Holbeck
581 Seats
27/07/14 – No film details advertised
18/05/40 – *Blind Alley*

PARKFIELD PICTURE PALACE, Jack
Lane, Hunslet
850 seats
17/08/14 – *The Wolf's Fang*
03/08/46 – *Patrick the Great*

PAVILION, Stanningley Road
644 seats
28/02/20 – *Daddy Longlegs*
05/04/70 – *Invitation to a Gunfighter*

PAVILION PICTURE PALACE,
Dewsbury Road
820 seats
04/08/11 – No film details advertised
29/09/56 – *Eye Witness*

PICTODROME, Wortley Road, Armley
540 seats
26/04/13 – *Nemesis*
13/09/58 – *Smiley Gets a Gun*

PICTODROME, Waterloo Road, Hunslet
504 seats
25/05/12 – No film details advertised
25/08/56 – *The Sword and the Rose*

PICTURE HOUSE, Town Street, Beeston
1083 seats
19/04/20 – *A Romance of Happy Valley*
04/07/59 – *Pale Arrow*

PICTURE HOUSE, Burley Road, Burley
616 seats
02/08/13 – No film details given
28/02/59 – *Passage Under the Sea*

PICTURE HOUSE, Domestic Street,
Holbeck
900 seats
05/01/16 – *My Old Dutch*
11/07/62 – *Two and Two Make Six*

PICTURE HOUSE, Harehills Corner,
Roundhay Road
900 seats
16/12/12 – *The Mine Owner*
05/10/63 – *Last Days of Pompeii*

PLAYHOUSE FILM THEATRE,
Calverley Street
700 Seats
27/09/70 – *The Kid Brother*
20/01/90 – Closed as a theatre

PLAZA, Wellington Street,
New Wortley
727 seats
17/04/30 – *Spite Marriage*
28/06/37 – *Spy of Napoleon*

PLAZA CINEMA; ASSEMBLY ROOMS,
New Briggate
1100 seats
15/04/07 – 'New Century talking and
singing pictures'
14/02/85 – *Hot and Blue*

PREMIER PICTURE PALACE, South
Accommodation Road, Hunslet
750 seats
04/12/12 – No film details advertised
30/11/52 – *Cry of the City*

PRINCESS CINEMA, Pontefract Lane,
Richmond Hill
964 seats
30/03/23 – No film details advertised
31/07/65 – *Roustabout*

QUEEN'S HALL PICTURE HOUSE,
Norfolk Street, Hunslet
250 seats
01/05/10 – No film details advertised
31/12/15 – No film details advertised

PLAZA CINEMA

LEEDS   Tel. 456882

FEBRUARY, 1975
Programmes Subject To Alteration

Above left: The original Plaza cinema in New Wortley.

Above right: A programme from the Plaza in New Briggate.

Left: The Princess cinema on Pontefract Lane.

Below: The Queen's.

The demolished Regal cinema in Crossgates.

The Pavilion in Hunslet.

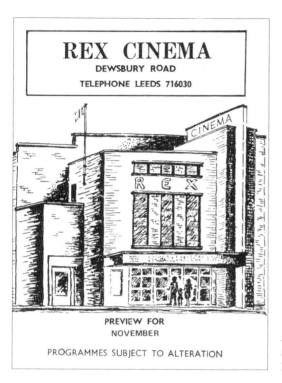

A programme from the Rex cinema. The films advertised included The Eiger Sanction *and* The Towering Inferno.

An aerial shot of the Royal cinema on Meanwood Road.

Left: *The frontage of the Shaftesbury cinema, with a poster advertising* The Magnificent Seven.

Below: *The Strand, photographed in July 1964.*

Right: *The much missed Tatler, Boar Lane.*

Below: *The Tivoli on Acre Road.*

TOWER
PICTURE HOUSE
NEW BRIGGATE
LEEDS

Tel,
28229

PROGRAMME
NOVEMBER - 1948

ENTERTAINMENT
FOR THE
DISCRIMINATING PICTUREGOER

ONE OF THE ASSOCIATED TOWER CINEMAS.

Right: *A programme for the Tower.*

Below: *The Victoria near York Road.*

QUEEN'S PICTURE THEATRE, Meadow
Road, Holbeck
Seats – as theatre 3,500, as cinema 916
Theatre opens 26/12/1898
Cinema from 01/12/24 – *The Covered Wagon*
19/10/57 – *Attila the Hun*

REGAL (from 06/01/30); PAVILION
PICTURE PALACE, Low Road, Hunslet
820 seats
06/01/13 – *Dante's Inferno*
30/05/59 – *In Love and War*

REGENT PICTURE HOUSE, Torre Road,
Burmantofts
1,076 seats
01/05/16 – *Both Sides of Life*
29/05/71 – *The Bounty Hunters*

REGAL SUPER CINEMA,
Cross Gates
1,500 seats
16/11/36 – *Strike Me Pink*
11/01/64 – *The Longest Day*

REX, Gypsy Lane, Beeston
1,350 seats
13/02/39 – *We're Going to be Rich*
28/02/76 – *The Apple Dumpling Gang*

RIALTO (from 04/02/27); PICTURE
HOUSE, Briggate
600 seats
04/04/11 – *Henry VIII*
11/03/39 – *Woman Teaser*

RITZ (from 05/10/38); PICTURE HOUSE,
Station Road, Crossgates
800 seats
05/08/20 – *Master of my Fate*
16/05/65 – *Hell to Eternity*

ROYAL (from 03/04/35); ATLAS,
Meanwood Road
345 seats
08/10/13 – No film details advertised
29/10/66 – *Girls! Girls! Girls!*

SAVOY, Queen's Arcade
250 seats
17/12/12 – No film details advertised
28/11/18 – No film details advertised

SCALA, Albion Place, Lands Lane
1692 seats
24/06/22 – *The Game of Life*
31/08/57 – *Across the Bridge*

SHAFTESBURY, York Road
1,603 seats
20/10/28 – *Beau Geste*
28/06/75 – *Death Wish*

SILVER ROYD ELECTRIC PICTURES,
Tong Road, Armley
290 seats
20/03/11 – No film details advertised
14/06/16 – No film details advertised

ST PETER'S PICTUREDROME, St Peter's
Street
350 seats
01/12/10 – No film details advertised
21/02/17 – No film details advertised

STAR SUPER CINEMA, Glenthorpe
Crescent, York Road
1,286 seats
21/02/38 – *Lost Horizon*
04/11/61 – *Secret Ways*

STER CENTURY CINEMAS; The Light,
The Headrow
13 screens
22/03/2002 – *Ice Age, Ali G In Da House,
Jimmy Neutron – Boy Genius, Return To
Neverland, Crossroads, Ali, A Beautiful Mind,
Don't Say a Word, Harry Potter, Lord of the
Rings, Monsters Inc, The Mothman Prophecies,
Ocean's 11, The Royal Tenenbaums, The Shipping
News, Thirteen Ghosts, We Were Soldiers*

STRAND, Jack Lane, Holbeck
1,166 seats
13/11/31 – *Plunder*
03/06/61 – *The Pure Hell of St Trinian's*

Lyons ICE CREAM

—completes the picture

TATLER; NEWS THEATRE;
ACADEMY; SAVOY; CITY, Boar Lane
514 seats
04/10/16 – *Beulah*
27/01/64 – *Sodom and Gomorrah*

THEATRE DE LUXE, Kirkgate
383 seats
03/12/10 – No film details advertised
26/05/34 – *Going Gay*

TIVOLI, Acre Road, Middleton
1,152 seats
21/05/34 – *A Bedtime Story*
01/05/60 – *I Was a Teenage Werewolf*
(Became the first Leeds cinema to start
bingo)

TOWER PICTURE HOUSE,
New Briggate
1,188 seats
12/04/20 – *The Kinsmen*
07/03/85 – *Codename: Wild Geese* and
Inglorious Bastards

VICTORIA, York Road
510 seats
25/10/12 – Licence granted
Demolished in 1937 to make way for the
new Star cinema

VICTORY, Camp Road, Woodhouse
811 seats
16/08/20 – *Mary Regan*
18/01/59 – *My Cousin Rachel*

VUE; WARNERS, Cardigan Fields,
Kirkstall Road
1,997 Seats over nine screens
16/07/98 – From 8.10 p.m. previews of
Godzilla
17/07/98 – From 10 a.m. *Godzilla, Grease,
Six Days Seven Nights, Mad City, City of
Angels, Barney's Great Adventure, The Wedding
Singer, Mimic, The Little Mermaid, Chubby
Brown Down Under*

WELLINGTON, Wellington Street
693 seats
09/11/20 – No film details advertised
05/11/41 – No film details advertised

WEST END; OK; COSY, Kirkstall Road
250 seats
09/09/11 – No film details advertised
28/12/12 – No film details advertised

nine

Roll-call for out of town cinemas

ALEXANDRA, Albion Street, Morley
(formerly the Empress Music Hall,
built 1908)
20/11/09 – Cinema shows begin
28/02/14 – Cinema shows cease

ALHAMBRA PICTURE HOUSE,
High Street, Kippax
442 seats
Opens 1913
Summer 1960 – *20,000 Leagues Under The Sea*

The CINEMA, Station Road, Garforth
394 seats
Opens 1913
04/06/66 – *Thunderball*

EMPIRE, Rawdon
570 seats
24/04/24 – *Fires of Fate* (films short-lived
– returned to stage shows until 1932)
11/02/56 – *A Stranger on Horseback* and
Slaves of Babylon

FILM THEATRE, RODNEY, RABY
PICTURE HOUSE, Caxton Street,
Wetherby
400 seats
21/04/15
25/04/64 – *4 For Texas*
Reopened as Film Theatre with 137 seats
15/07/94 – *Four Weddings and a Funeral*

GEM PICTURES (from 26/08/60);
TEMPERANCE HALL PICTURES,
Kirk Lane, Yeadon
524 seats
22/12/11 – 'Electric Pictures'
12/06/63 – *300 Spartans*

GLENROYAL, New Road Side,
Horsforth
900 seats
01/11/37 – *Michael Strogoff*
08/02/64 – *The VIPs*

IMPERIAL, Town Street, Horsforth
541 seats

Original Imperial 1911
New Imperial 1925
25/06/60 – *Please Don't Eat the Daisies*

PALACE; ELECTRIC PICTURE
PALACE AND VARIETIES, Lowtown,
Pudsey
19/12/10 – No film details advertised
30/07/60 – *Odongo*

PALACE PICTURES, Town Hall, Yeadon
11/11/12 – Short-lived use of Town Hall
as cinema

PAVILION, South Queen Street, Morley
(formerly the New Pavilion Theatre)
777 seats
17/03/13 – Cinema shows during stage
renovation after fire
27/07/68 – *Beach Red and Operation Kid
Brother*

PLAZA; PICTURE PALACE, Town
Street, Guiseley
02/08/12 – 'The latest Pictures from
London'
04/04/59 – *No Time to Die*

PICTURE HOUSE, Church Lane, Pudsey
901 seats
22/11/20 – *Darby and Joan*
12/11/60 – *Doctor in Love*

PICTURE HOUSE, Queen Street, Morley
959 Seats
02/02/14 – *Dante's Inferno*
06/02/60 – *The Siege of Pinchgut*

PICTURE PALACE, Rothwell
900 seats
Closed 14/06/58

RIALTO, PICTURE HOUSE, Town
Street, Rodley
650 seats
24/10/27 – *The Triumph of the Rat*
07/07/56 – *One Desire*

THE
CINEMA

TEL. 2600   GARFORTH   TEL. 2600

WEEK COMMENCING SUNDAY, MAY 29th, 1966

— FOR SEVEN DAYS

HERE COMES THE BIGGEST BOND OF ALL

THUNDERBALL

SEAN CONNERY
007

The final film at Garforth's Cinema.

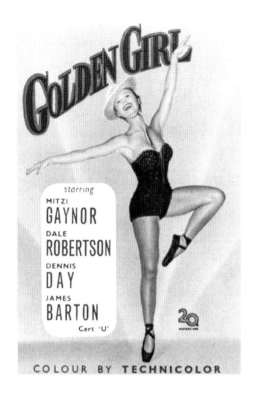

Above: A Pathé Super Gazette ('The World's Greatest Current News Film') postcard with a piece of dark celluloid in the centre for watching the eclipse on 29 June 1927.

Left: *An advert for* Golden Girl, *starring Mitzi Gaynor, running for three days at the Carlton Cinema, Carlton Hill.*

RITZ, Aberford Road, Woodlesford
500 seats
Closed 18/12/71

ROYAL, Bradford Road, Stanningley
250 seats
06/03/11 – No film details advertised
14/11/31 – *Show of Shows*

SAVOY, Bradford Road, Stanningley
1000 seats
17/09/37 – *Café Collette*
25/09/65 – *How the West Was Won*

SHOWCASE, Birstall
3400 seats

Opens 15/12/89 – *Back to the Future 2, Dead Poets Society, Ghostbusters 2, The Dream Team, Oliver and Company, Cat Chaser, The Wolves of Willoughby Chase, Wilt, Shirley Valentine, Field of Dreams, Pet Sematary*
Two new screens open 12/2/93 adding 300 seats
Stay Tuned, Night at the City

STUDIO 1 and 2; PICTURE HOUSE, Town Street, Yeadon
801 seats
03/08/25 – *The Man Who Came Back*
30/10/86 – *Cinderella, Poltergeist 2 – The Other Side*

Further reading

Allen Eyles, *ABC: The First Name in Entertainment* (1993)

Louis Mannix, *Memories of a Cinema Man* (1993)

Geoff J. Mellor, *The Picture Pioneers* (1971)

Geoff J. Mellor, *Movie Makers and Picture Palaces* (1996)

David M. Ryder, *Rise and Fall of the Rawdon Empire* (1995)

Robert E. Preedy, *Leeds Cinemas Remembered* (1980)

— *Leeds Cinemas 2* (1982)

— *That'll be the Day in Leeds* (1984)

— *Flicks – The cinemas of Leeds and Bradford* (1994)

— 'The Cinemas of Leeds', in *Aspects of Leeds (1998)*

— 'Claude Whincup biography', in *Aspects of Leeds 2 (1999)*

— *Batley Variety Club* (2003)

Other local titles published by Tempus

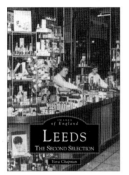

Leeds: The Second Selection
VERA CHAPMAN

In this superb collection of images, historic Leeds is once again revealed to the reader through a remarkable selection of postcards and archive photographs drawn from the author's personal collection. This volume will delight those who know the area, and evoke memories of former times for all those who have lived and experienced life here over the years.

0 7524 2650 8

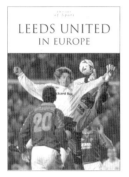

Leeds United in Europe
DAVID SAFFER AND HOWARD DAPIN

From their first steps in Europe in the mid-1960s during the revolutionary Don Revie era, to Champions League football, Leeds have been a force to be reckoned with in European competition. This evocative collection of action shots, team groups, programme covers and cartoons illustrates the history of United through the triumphs and disappointments of epic struggles against the best teams on the Continent.

0 7524 2043 7

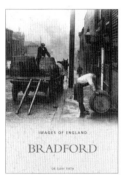

Bradford
DR GARY FIRTH

J.B. Priestley once wrote that 'Bradford is a vast series of pictures, in time and space; it is a one hundred thousand succeeding states of mind.' This selection of more than 200 archive photographs is an attempt to tap into Priestley's mental pictures – the many facets of Bradford during the period from 1880 to the 1950s. These fascinating photographs should evoke reminiscences of buildings and streets long gone and stir memories of Bradford residents going about their work and play in this busy, vibrant city.

0 7524 3019 X

Sheffield Cinemas
CLIFFORD SHAW

The first purpose-built cinema in Sheffield was the Picture Palace in Union Street, which opened in 1910. By the outbreak of war in 1914, there were thirty cinemas either completed or under construction. Cinemas suffered a slump during the 1920s but were revived by the advent of the 'talkies' in 1929/30. This pictorial compilation places on record some of the history of local cinemas; hopefully it will be a reminder of what once was.

0 7524 2293 X

If you are interested in purchasing other books published by Tempus, or in case you have difficulty finding any Tempus books in your local bookshop, you can also place orders directly through our website

www.tempus-publishing.com